LEVELED
Readers' Theater

Grade 3

Editorial Development: De Gibbs
                       Camille Liscinsky
                       Lisa Vitarisi Mathews
        Copy Editing: Carrie Gwynne
       Art Direction: Kathy Kopp
                       Cheryl Puckett
        Illustration: David Schimmell
        Cover Design: Cheryl Puckett
   Design/Production: Arynne Elfenbein
                       Yuki Meyer
                       Marcia Smith

EMC 3483

Helping Children Learn since 1979

**Congratulations on your
purchase of some of the
finest teaching materials
in the world.**

Visit *teaching-standards.com* to view a
correlation of this book's activities to your
state's standards. This is a free service.

Contents

Introduction

Scripts and Activities

What's in Every Unit?

1 A teacher resource page guides instruction.

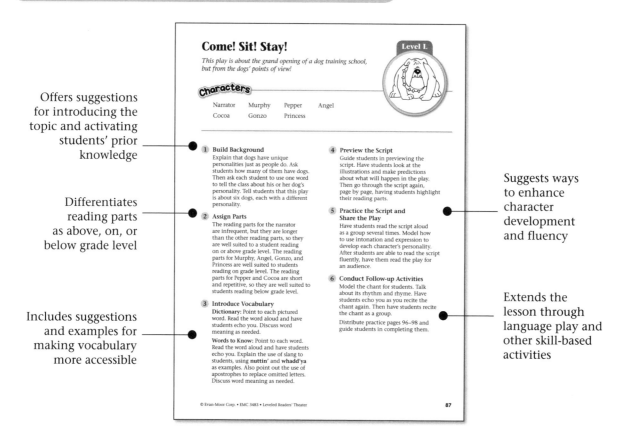

Offers suggestions for introducing the topic and activating students' prior knowledge

Differentiates reading parts as above, on, or below grade level

Includes suggestions and examples for making vocabulary more accessible

Suggests ways to enhance character development and fluency

Extends the lesson through language play and other skill-based activities

Come! Sit! Stay!

This play is about the grand opening of a dog training school, but from the dogs' points of view!

Level L

Characters

| Narrator | Murphy | Pepper | Angel |
| Cocoa | Gonzo | Princess | |

1 Build Background
Explain that dogs have unique personalities just as people do. Ask students how many of them have dogs. Then ask each student to use one word to tell the class about his or her dog's personality. Tell students that this play is about six dogs, each with a different personality.

2 Assign Parts
The reading parts for the narrator are infrequent, but they are longer than the other reading parts, so they are well suited to a student reading on or above grade level. The reading parts for Murphy, Angel, Gonzo, and Princess are well suited to students reading on grade level. The reading parts for Pepper and Cocoa are short and repetitive, so they are well suited to students reading below grade level.

3 Introduce Vocabulary
Dictionary: Point to each pictured word. Read the word aloud and have students echo you. Discuss word meaning as needed.

Words to Know: Point to each word. Read the word aloud and have students echo you. Explain the use of slang to students, using **nuttin'** and **whadd'ya** as examples. Also point out the use of apostrophes to replace omitted letters. Discuss word meaning as needed.

4 Preview the Script
Guide students in previewing the script. Have students look at the illustrations and make predictions about what will happen in the play. Then go through the script again, page by page, having students highlight their reading parts.

5 Practice the Script and Share the Play
Have students read the script aloud as a group several times. Model how to use intonation and expression to develop each character's personality. After students are able to read the script fluently, have them read the play for an audience.

6 Conduct Follow-up Activities
Model the chant for students. Talk about its rhythm and rhyme. Have students echo you as you recite the chant again. Then have students recite the chant as a group.

Distribute practice pages 96–98 and guide students in completing them.

© Evan-Moor Corp. • EMC 3483 • Leveled Readers' Theater   87

2 A reproducible dictionary page introduces vocabulary from the script.

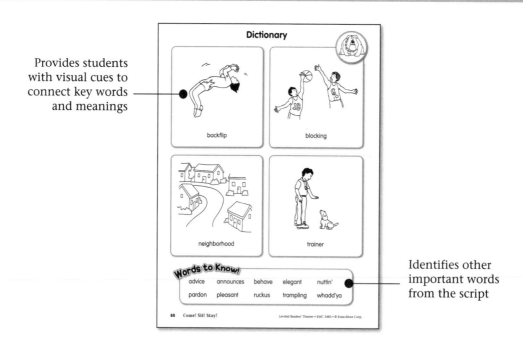

Provides students with visual cues to connect key words and meanings

Identifies other important words from the script

Dictionary

backflip

blocking

neighborhood

trainer

Words to Know!

| advice | announces | behave | elegant | nuttin' |
| pardon | pleasant | ruckus | trampling | whadd'ya |

88   Come! Sit! Stay!   Leveled Readers' Theater • EMC 3483 • © Evan-Moor Corp.

3 A reproducible minibook script is designed especially for students in the primary grades.

Easy assembly:
• Reproduce script pages.
• Cut along dotted lines.
• Staple into a minibook.

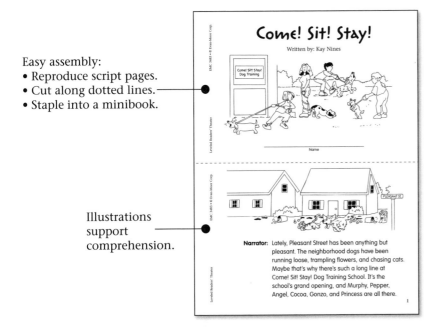

Illustrations support comprehension.

Size and orientation make it easy to handle.

4 A reproducible chant provides additional fluency practice.

5 Reproducible activity pages reinforce vocabulary and comprehension.

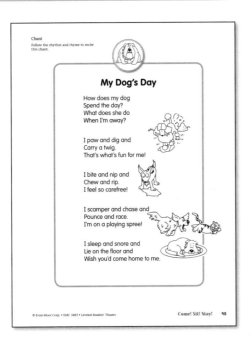

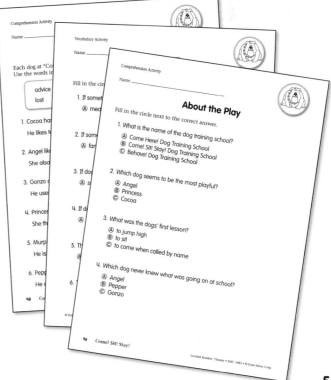

Using the Leveled Scripts to Increase Reading Fluency

The National Reading Panel identifies fluency as a key component of reading instruction because of its impact on students' reading efficacy and comprehension. The *Leveled Readers' Theater* format provides a platform for fun, repeated readings that build students' reading fluency.

About the Reading Levels

Each play has been assigned a Guided Reading level (J–N) based on factors related to accessibility. The factors considered in leveling the scripts are:

- Text structure, such as plot, cause/effect, and problem/solution
- Text features, such as repetition, point of view, and dialogue
- Vocabulary
- Sentence complexity
- Illustration to text match
- Book and print features
- Genre and topic

Enhance Your Core Reading Program

You can use the leveled scripts as a supplement to your core reading program. The scripts provide a motivating resource that offers purposeful reading practice for students at many different reading levels. Assemble reading groups that include a range of ability levels so that more skilled readers can model fluency to less skilled readers. The engaging, relevant topics in *Leveled Readers' Theater* scripts will entertain and interest reluctant readers and provide fluent readers with the opportunity to explore and enjoy a variety of genres and characters.

Support English Language Learners

The *Leveled Readers' Theater* scripts provide a reading experience that can increase confidence and transform English Language Learners into fluent readers. The teacher resource pages and follow-up activities that accompany every unit provide the necessary support and scaffolding for effective instruction to EL students in the areas of reading, writing, listening, and speaking.

How to Present a Unit

Choose a leveled script that contains reading parts written at students' instructional reading levels. Use the teacher resource page to conduct guided instruction lessons that help students understand the topic and become comfortable with the format of the script. Start slowly and engage students in repeated readings, modeling fluency often, so that students gain confidence reading the script aloud. Support students by modeling reading strategies, such as using context clues, identifying word structure, and identifying letter-sound relationships. Use the follow-up vocabulary and comprehension activity pages as informal assessments to gauge students' understanding of the play.

Leveled Readers' Theater • EMC 3483 • © Evan-Moor Corp.

Silly States

This play consists of rhyming verses that include puns on eleven states' names.

Reader 1   Reader 2   Reader 3   Reader 4

---

1 Build Background

Explain to students that this play contains puns. Write the following two puns on the board: "When a clock is hungry, it goes back four seconds." "A bicycle can't stand on its own because it is two-tired." Tell students that a pun is a phrase that deliberately confuses the use of similar sounding words and homophones in order to be humorous. Discuss the puns you wrote on the board.

2 Assign Parts

Although the script calls for four readers, any number of readers may be used. You might even consider having each verse read by a different student. This play is well suited to students reading on or below grade level.

3 Introduce Vocabulary

Dictionary: Point to each pictured word. Read the word aloud and have students echo you. Discuss word meaning as needed.

Words to Know: Point to each word. Read the word aloud and have students echo you. Remind students that the vowel pair **oi** in the word **joined** sounds like /oy/. Teach the word **quota** as a sight word. You might want to remind students that dividing a word into syllables can help them pronounce it. In the word **quota**, for example, the syllable division (quo•ta) indicates a long o sound. Discuss word meaning as needed.

4 Preview the Script

Guide students in previewing the script. Have students look at the illustrations and make predictions about what is happening in each picture. Then go through the script again, page by page, having students highlight their reading parts. Point out the words in each pun that make up a state's name.

5 Practice the Script and Share the Play

Have students read the script aloud as a group several times. Model how to use intonation and expression to emphasize the rhymes and the names of the states. After students are able to read the script fluently, have them read the play for an audience.

6 Conduct Follow-up Activities

Model the chant for students. Talk about its rhythm and rhyme. Have students echo you as you recite the chant again. Then have students recite the chant as a group.

Distribute practice pages 16–18 and guide students in completing them.

Dictionary

fair

jersey

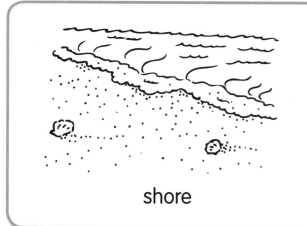

shore

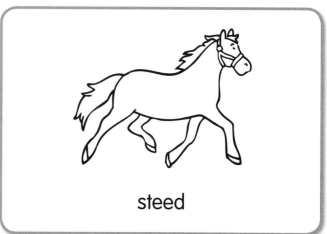

steed

sundaes

yawn

Words to Know!

bothersome	disagreed	exercise	joined
nickname	quota	soared	water-ski

Leveled Readers' Theater • EMC 3483 • © Evan-Moor Corp.

EMC 3483 • © Evan-Moor Corp.

Leveled Readers' Theater

Silly States

Written by: Ken Tuckee

Name _____

EMC 3483 • © Evan-Moor Corp.

Leveled Readers' Theater

Reader 1: If Mary sailed out to sea,
Away from shore and sand,
I'd like to know—can you tell me—
Just where would Mary land?

1

Reader 2: We ate a yummy dinner,
And then I saw Ora yawn.
It's time to do the dishes.
Now where has Ora gone?

2

Reader 3: An English lady had a steed.
She called him 'ighland Bay.
He needed exercise,
So she rode 'ighland every day.

3

Reader 4: Two sisters disagreed
About the garden chores,
and so I said,
"My dears, let Lily rake,
And just let Ida hoe."

4

Reader 1: Tenny was a pilot who
Soared over land and sea.
There up in the air, I wonder,
What did Tenny see?

5

Reader 2: On vacation at the lake,
Mike tried to water-ski.
He dropped the rope and took a spill.
Now he's in misery.

6

Reader 3: Young Della went out shopping.
She bought jeans for the fair.
She dropped them in a puddle.
Oh no! What will Della wear?

7

Reader 4: When Harry eats his ice cream,
Three large sundaes is his quota.
When he's just a little thirsty,
Harry drinks a mini-soda.

8

Reader 1: When Jason joined the football team,
He was a skinny guy.
Now, ten pizzas later,
A new jersey he must buy.

9

Reader 2: My brother Ill is a pest at school.
In class, he's a bothersome boy.
When we get home each day,
Mom asks, "So, who did Ill annoy?"

10

Reader 3: "Oh" is my friend's nickname.
She's the only Oh I know.
When I'm surprised to see her,
I shout out, "Oh, hi Oh!"

11

Let's Hear It for the States!

Toot a horn for Arizona!
Give a toast to Idaho!
Shout out for Louisiana!
Now cheer on New Mexico!

Turn cartwheels for Ohio!
Clap your hands for Kentucky!
Dance a reel for West Virginia!
Play the drums for New Jersey!

Tip your top hat to Rhode Island!
Run a race for Tennessee!
Twirl around for North Dakota!
Raise the flag for Hawaii!

Name _____

About the Play

Fill in the circle next to the correct answer.

1. The play uses the names of states _____.

   Ⓐ to explain where they are
   Ⓑ in funny puns that rhyme
   Ⓒ in alphabetical order

2. What is Harry's quota of ice-cream sundaes?

   Ⓐ three
   Ⓑ four
   Ⓒ five

3. Which words tell about the boy named Ill?

   Ⓐ quiet, shy
   Ⓑ a pest, bothersome
   Ⓒ sad, upset

4. Why did Jason buy a new football jersey?

   Ⓐ He ate too many ice-cream sundaes.
   Ⓑ He joined a new team.
   Ⓒ He ate too many pizzas.

Name _____

I Know the Words

Fill in the circle next to the correct answer.

1. What does a **steed** need?

   Ⓐ gas   Ⓑ oil   Ⓒ exercise

2. What is at the **shore**?

   Ⓐ books   Ⓑ sand   Ⓒ corn

3. What do you do with a **sundae**?

   Ⓐ sail it   Ⓑ water-ski in it   Ⓒ eat it

4. What do you do when you are **thirsty**?

   Ⓐ drink something   Ⓑ go shopping   Ⓒ brush your teeth

5. What does a **pest** do?

   Ⓐ bothers people   Ⓑ sells books   Ⓒ water-skis

6. What is a **nickname**?

   Ⓐ a pet   Ⓑ a vacation   Ⓒ a shortened name

Name _____

I Know Which State

Write the correct state's name to complete each pun.

> Delaware   Idaho   Illinois
>
> Maryland   New Jersey   Tennessee

1. If Mary sailed out to sea, away from shore and sand,

   I'd like to know—can you tell me—just where would _____?

2. Tenny was a pilot who soared over land and sea.

   There up in the air, I wonder, what did _____?

3. When Jason joined the football team, he was a skinny guy.

   Now, ten pizzas later, a _____ he must buy.

4. My brother Ill is a pest at school. In class, he's a bothersome boy. When

   we get home each day, Mom asks, "So, who did _____?"

5. Two sisters disagreed about the garden chores, and so I said,

   "My dears, let Lily rake, and just let _____."

6. Young Della went out shopping. She bought jeans for the fair.

   She dropped them in a puddle. Oh no! What will _____?

Stuck in the Middle

This play is about a boy who is unhappy about being the middle child in his family.

Characters

Evan   Dad   Dillon   Mom

---

1 Build Background

Discuss with students what it's like to have brothers and sisters. Talk about being the youngest child, the oldest child, and the middle child. Invite students to share their experiences and opinions. Tell students that this play is about a boy who feels "stuck" as a middle child.

2 Assign Parts

All of the reading parts in this play are well suited to students reading on grade level. The reading parts for Evan are the most frequent. The reading parts for Dad, Mom, and Dillon are less frequent than Evan's but are comparable to each other.

3 Introduce Vocabulary

Dictionary: Point to each pictured word. Read the word aloud and have students echo you. Remind students that the letters **eigh** in the word **neighborhood** sound like /ā/. Discuss word meaning as needed.

Words to Know: Point to each word. Read the word aloud and have students echo you. Point out that several of the vocabulary words are compound words. Discuss word meaning as needed.

4 Preview the Script

Guide students in previewing the script. Have students look at the illustrations and make predictions about what will happen in the play. Then go through the script again, page by page, having students highlight their reading parts.

5 Practice the Script and Share the Play

Have students read the script aloud as a group several times. Model how to use intonation and expression to convey frustration, concern, and surprise. After students are able to read the script fluently, have them read the play for an audience.

6 Conduct Follow-up Activities

Model the chant for students. Talk about its rhythm and rhyme. Have students echo you as you recite the chant again. Then have students recite the chant as a group.

Distribute practice pages 28–30 and guide students in completing them.

Dictionary

garbage cans

neighborhood

newspapers

skateboard

Words to Know!

chores	computer	curb	deliver
downtown	hardworking	meantime	youngest

Stuck in the Middle

Written by: Mona N. Groner

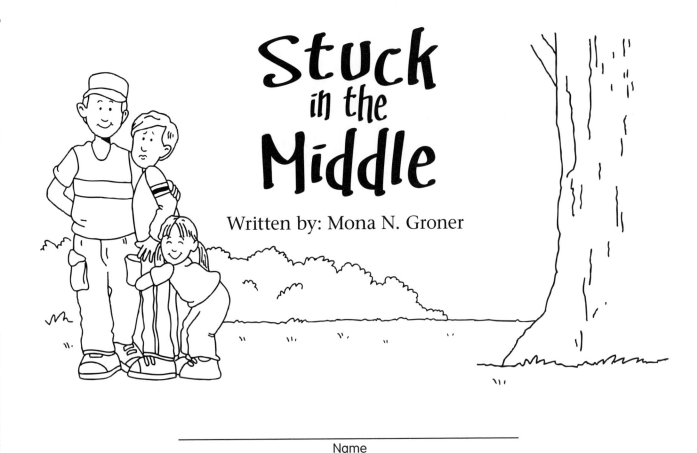

_____
Name

Evan: There are three children in my family. My big brother's name is Dillon, my little sister's name is Emma, and my name is Evan. I'm not the oldest, and I'm not the youngest. I'm in the middle. I hate being stuck in the middle. If you lived at our house, you'd know why.

1

Dad: Ev–an! Help me take the garbage cans out to the curb, please.

Evan: I'm on the computer, Dad. Can't Dillon help you?

Dillon: I've gotta go to work now, little brother. Gotta deliver those newspapers on time. See ya later.

Dad: Ev–an! Are you coming?

Evan: Be there in a minute, Dad.

Mom: Evan, Dad has to go to the dentist in a few minutes. I'll take Emma with me to the neighborhood meeting. By the way, where is Emma?

Evan: I haven't seen her. I've gotta go help Dad. And then I want to get back to my computer game.

Mom: Oh no! What happened in here? Ev–an!

Evan: What's wrong, Mom?

Mom: Emma got paint all over the kitchen—and all over herself! I have to go, Evan. You'll have to clean up this mess.

4

Evan: But, Mom …

Mom: Please, Evan! I have to get to the meeting. Dillon will be home soon. He can help you take care of Emma. Bye!

Evan: I have to do everything. It's not fair!

5

Dillon: Hi, I'm home!

Evan: Sure, now you're home. Now that I've cleaned up all of Emma's mess.

Dillon: What mess?

Evan: Never mind. Mom said you have to help me watch Emma.

Dillon: Okay—in a minute. First, I want to count my money. I got paid today. I'm pretty sure I have enough to buy a Fearless Flyer skateboard!

- -

Evan: That's not fair! I do all the work around here, and you're the one making money! I have to take out the garbage! I have to help clean the house! I even have to watch Emma!

Dillon: I'm sorry I can't help, but I have a job now.

Evan: Yeah, you have a job, Emma's too little, and Mom and Dad are busy. So I have to do everything. It's not fair! I hate being stuck in the middle!

Dad: Hello boys … I'm back. What's going on? Evan, are you crying? Dillon, what happened?

Dillon: Nothing, Dad. He's just feeling stuck in the middle.

- -

Dad: Stuck in the middle? Dillon, watch Emma while I talk to Evan for a few minutes.

Dillon: Sure, Dad.

Dad: Come on, Evan. Tell me why you're so upset.

Evan: It's just that Dillon gets paid for working, and I don't. Now he can buy a Fearless Flyer. I do just as much work as he does, but I can't buy a Fearless Flyer.

Mom: Hi everybody … I'm home. What's wrong, Evan?

Dad: Evan wants to work like Dillon so he can buy a Fearless Flyer skateboard.

Evan: I already work! Since Dillon got a job, I do almost all the chores. And Emma is too young to help.

Mom: You're right, Evan. You've been helping out a lot around here.

Dad: I think maybe Mom and I need to make some changes.

Mom: I agree. Let's sit down tomorrow and talk about it. In the meantime, let's all go downtown.

Evan and Dad: What for?

Mom: I think Skater World has two Fearless Flyers waiting for our hardworking boys!

Evan: No way! Really? Thanks, Mom! I'll go get Dillon!

Being in the Middle

If I were a sandwich cookie
(And I believe you will agree),
The layer in the middle
Is the one I'd want to be.

If I rode a roller coaster
With my best friends, Jim and Joe,
I'd want to sit between them.
It's the safest spot I know.

And when I eat a hot dog,
The main reason for the bun
Is to hold in all the fixin's
That make a hot dog fun.

So being in the middle
Is not so bad, you see.
I guess I should be happy
That the middle child is me!

Name _____

About the Play

Fill in the circle next to the correct answer.

1. Why is Evan stuck "in the middle"?

    Ⓐ His little sister gets into trouble.
    Ⓑ He doesn't have his own room.
    Ⓒ He isn't the oldest, and he isn't the youngest.

2. What does Dillon want to do before he helps watch Emma?

    Ⓐ count his money
    Ⓑ eat lunch
    Ⓒ buy a Fearless Flyer skateboard

3. What is Evan upset about?

    Ⓐ He wants a job delivering newspapers.
    Ⓑ He wants his own room.
    Ⓒ He does all the chores by himself.

4. At the end of the play, Evan's parents say they will _____.

    Ⓐ give Evan his own room
    Ⓑ make some changes
    Ⓒ hire a baby sitter

Name _____

I Know the Words

Fill in the circle next to the correct answer.

1. The word **deliver** can mean _____.

   Ⓐ to see   Ⓑ to bring   Ⓒ to write

2. A **hardworking** person _____.

   Ⓐ hardly works   Ⓑ works a little   Ⓒ works a lot

3. A **neighborhood** is a place with _____.

   Ⓐ one house   Ⓑ many houses   Ⓒ no houses

4. A **downtown** area usually has _____.

   Ⓐ many houses   Ⓑ a forest   Ⓒ stores and offices

5. If you are doing **chores**, you are _____.

   Ⓐ watching TV   Ⓑ doing small jobs Ⓒ talking on the phone

6. If you take something to the **curb**, you take it to the _____.

   Ⓐ dentist   Ⓑ backyard   Ⓒ edge of the sidewalk

Name _____

I Know What Happened

Look at each picture. Write sentences to tell what happened in the play.

1. _____

_____

_____

_____

_____

2. _____

_____

_____

_____

_____

3. _____

_____

_____

_____

_____

How Hippos Came to Live in Water

This play is based on an African folk tale about how hippos came to live in water.

Characters

Storyteller   Hippo Chief   Hippo Princesses

Giraffe Chief   Cheetah Chief

1 Build Background

Tell students that a folk tale is a story that has been handed down from generation to generation. Explain that many folk tales are meant to amuse listeners and that they often humorously explain something that happens in nature. Tell students that this play is based on a folk tale about hippopotamuses.

2 Assign Parts

The reading parts for the storyteller are the most lengthy and include some complex sentence structures, so they are well suited to a student reading on or above grade level. The reading parts for Hippo Chief are well suited to a student reading on grade level. The reading parts for Giraffe Chief and Cheetah Chief are both short and contain simple vocabulary, so they are well suited to students reading on or below grade level. The reading parts for the Hippo Princesses are read chorally and are also well suited to students reading on or below grade level.

3 Introduce Vocabulary

Dictionary: Point to each pictured word. Read the word aloud and have students echo you. Point out that the letter **h** at the end of **cheetah** is silent. Discuss word meaning as needed.

Words to Know: Point to each word. Read the word aloud and have students echo you. Remind students how to pronounce the vowel digraph in the word **chief** and the r-controlled vowels in the words **overheard** and **search**. Discuss word meaning as needed.

4 Preview the Script

Guide students in previewing the script. Have students look at the illustrations and make predictions about what will happen in the play. Then go through the script again, page by page, having students highlight their reading parts.

5 Practice the Script and Share the Play

Have students read the script aloud as a group several times. Model how to use intonation and expression to develop each character's personality. After students are able to read the script fluently, have them read the play for an audience.

6 Conduct Follow-up Activities

Model the chant for students. Recite it as you would a series of limericks. Have students echo you as you recite the chant again. Then have students recite the chant as a group.

Distribute practice pages 42–44 and guide students in completing them.

Dictionary

 backside

 cheetah

 giraffe

 grassland

 hippo

 hut

Words to Know!

chief	graze	imagine	invited	mighty
overheard	princesses	search	squeeze	tugging

Leveled Readers' Theater • EMC 3483 • © Evan-Moor Corp.

EMC 3483 • © Evan-Moor Corp.

How Hippos Came to Live in Water

Written by: Tori Teller

_____

Name

EMC 3483 • © Evan-Moor Corp.

Storyteller: Once upon a time, hippos lived on land. One hippo was a mighty chief. The chief had seven sisters. Each one was a hippo princess. As you can imagine, the hut the hippo chief and his sisters lived in was very crowded.

1

Hippo Chief: There are too many hippos in this hut! We are getting larger, and the hut is getting smaller. A chief should have plenty of room, but I could never ask my sisters to leave.

2

Storyteller: The next day, the chief overheard his sisters talking.

Hippo Princesses: We are hippo princesses. We need more room! We wish we could live in a larger place, but we cannot leave our brother.

3

Storyteller: Hippo Chief could not believe his luck. His sisters wanted more room, too!

Hippo Chief: I need a plan. I don't want my sisters to think I want them to leave the hut. I will visit some of the grassland chiefs. They will help me think of a plan.

Storyteller: The next day, Hippo Chief left the hut early in the morning, before the sun got too hot. He walked to Giraffe Chief's field.

Giraffe Chief: Hippo Chief, why are you visiting me so early in the morning?

4

Hippo Chief: I have a problem. My seven sisters are getting bigger, and our hut seems to be getting smaller.

Giraffe Chief: What can I do to help you?

Hippo Chief: I can't search for a new home for them, because the sun is too hot during the day. Would you please search the grasslands for a home that is large enough for seven hippo princesses?

Giraffe Chief: I'll begin my search right away.

5

Hippo Chief: But remember, my sisters cannot stay in the hot sun. The place you find must be cool.

Storyteller: Next, Hippo Chief paid a visit to Cheetah Chief and told him the same thing he had told Giraffe Chief.

Cheetah Chief: The hippo princesses are very big. Must they all live together?

Hippo Chief: They will be lost without me, so they must at least have each other.

Cheetah Chief: Very well. I'll begin my search right away.

6

Storyteller: Hippo Chief hurried home to the shade of his hut.

Hippo Princesses: Brother, where did you go so early this morning?

Hippo Chief: Cheetah Chief and Giraffe Chief needed my help. I need to rest now. The sun made me very tired.

Hippo Princesses: Oh yes, dear brother, come in out of the sun.

Hippo Chief: Um, can you move over a bit? I cannot quite fit through the door.

7

Hippo Princesses: Oh dear! Well, yes. Let's move over, princesses! Ow, oof, grr, mmm … Squeeze together a little more. There we are. Are you all the way in, Brother?

8

Storyteller: Hippo Chief could not bear to tell his sisters that he was not all the way in. His backside was still sticking out of the hut. A little later in the day, Hippo Chief felt something tugging at his tail.

Cheetah Chief: Hippo Chief, it's me, Cheetah Chief. Giraffe Chief and I are here to talk to you.

9

Storyteller: Hippo Chief carefully backed out of the little hut. He spoke in a whisper.

Hippo Chief: Did you find a place for the hippo princesses to live?

Cheetah Chief: We found a place where they can be out of the hot sun. And it's big enough for all of them to be together.

10

Hippo Chief: That's wonderful! Thank you. But now, how will I get them to live there?

Giraffe Chief: Tell the hippo princesses that you are all invited to enjoy the shade under my tree at one o'clock this afternoon. That's the hottest time of the day.

Storyteller: Hippo Chief thanked his friends for their help and squeezed his body back into the hut. He told his sisters about the invitation.

Hippo Princesses: How wonderful! We must not be late!

11

Storyteller: A little before one o'clock, Hippo Chief and the seven hippo princesses made their way to the shade under Giraffe Chief's tree. The sun was very hot, and the princesses were tired when they arrived.

Giraffe Chief: Stand in the shade, Hippo Princesses. Graze on the grass. Do you feel that cool breeze?

12

Hippo Princesses: Yes, it is nice and cool under your tree. Much cooler than in our tiny hut.

Hippo Chief: It's time for us to walk home now, sisters. Too bad the sun will still be hot.

Cheetah Chief: Don't worry. I know a cool place where you can stop and rest on the way.

13

Storyteller: Cheetah Chief and Giraffe Chief led the hippos to a river and invited them to go into it.

Hippo Princesses: Go into the river? But we'll get wet.

Hippo Chief: Watch me, sisters. It is cool in … ahhh. Oh, this water feels good!

14

Storyteller: One by one, all seven hippo princesses went into the cool river. It felt so good, and they had so much room that they didn't want to go back to their little hut ever again. As it turns out, neither did Hippo Chief. And that is how hippos came to live in water.

15

The Strange Hippo

A strange creature is the hippo.
It certainly is tubby.
Its body's huge.
It weighs two tons.
But its legs are short and stubby!

An odd name is *hippopotamus.*
"River horse" is what it means.
But it has no mane
And can't win a race.
It has whale in its genes.

A huge creature is the hippo.
Though third largest beast on land,
It lives in water
And sometimes bathes in mud.
As a swimmer, it's quite grand!

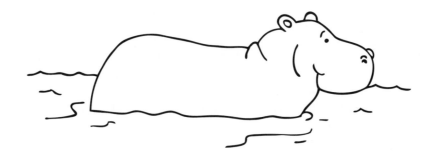

Name _____

About the Play

Fill in the circle next to the correct answer.

1. Where did Hippo Chief and the hippo princesses live first?

   Ⓐ They lived under a tree.
   Ⓑ They lived in a hut.
   Ⓒ They lived in a cave.

2. Why did the hippos want to live somewhere else?

   Ⓐ They were too crowded.
   Ⓑ They were too cold.
   Ⓒ They were too hot.

3. Why didn't Hippo Chief and the hippo princesses talk to each other about how they were feeling?

   Ⓐ They did not want to hurt one another's feelings.
   Ⓑ They did not like to talk during the day.
   Ⓒ They did not live near each other.

4. Why did Hippo Chief decide to stay with the hippo princesses?

   Ⓐ He missed them too much.
   Ⓑ He liked the cool water and all the room in the river.
   Ⓒ His hut burned down.

Name _____

I Know the Words

Fill in the circle next to the correct answer.

1. To **overhear** something means to _____.

   Ⓐ see it   Ⓑ know it   Ⓒ hear it

2. To **search** for something means to _____.

   Ⓐ ask for it   Ⓑ look for it   Ⓒ reach for it

3. If something is **mighty**, it is _____.

   Ⓐ powerful   Ⓑ weak   Ⓒ tiny

4. If something is **tugging**, it is _____.

   Ⓐ talking   Ⓑ pulling   Ⓒ yelling

5. When you **squeeze** something, you _____.

   Ⓐ hold it gently Ⓑ step on it   Ⓒ press it firmly

6. To be a **chief** means to be _____.

   Ⓐ a student   Ⓑ a leader   Ⓒ an animal

Name _____

I Know What Happened

Look at each picture. Write sentences to tell what happened in the play.

1. _____

_____

_____

_____

_____

2. _____

_____

_____

_____

_____

3. _____

_____

_____

_____

_____

Young King Cole

This play is about how King Cole became a merry old soul.

Characters

Storyteller	Queen	King	Jester
Cackle	Chuckle	Snort	

1 Build Background

Read the nursery rhyme *Old King Cole* (below) to students. Then explain that they will read a play about King Cole when he was young.

Old King Cole

Old King Cole was a merry old soul,
  and a merry old soul was he.
He called for his pipe,
  he called for his bowl,
And he called for his fiddlers three.

Every fiddler had a fine fiddle,
  and a very fine fiddle had he.
Oh, there's none so rare
  as can compare
With King Cole and his fiddlers three.

2 Assign Parts

The reading parts for the storyteller are frequent and are well suited to a student reading on or above grade level. The reading parts for the queen, the king, and the jester are short and simple, so they are well suited to students reading on or below grade level. The reading parts for Cackle, Chuckle, and Snort contain relatively complex sentences and are well suited to students reading on or above grade level.

3 Introduce Vocabulary

Dictionary: Point to each pictured word. Read the word aloud and have students echo you. Discuss word meaning as needed.

Words to Know: Point to each word. Read the word aloud and have students echo you. Remind students how to pronounce the vowel digraphs in the words **certainly**, **instead**, **laugh** and **soul**. Discuss word meaning as needed.

4 Preview the Script

Guide students in previewing the script. Have students look at the illustrations and make predictions about what will happen in the play. Then go through the script again, page by page, having students highlight their reading parts.

5 Practice the Script and Share the Play

Have students read the script aloud as a group several times. Model how to use intonation and expression to develop each character's personality. After students are able to read the script fluently, have them read the play for an audience.

6 Conduct Follow-up Activities

Model the chant for students. Talk about its rhythm and rhyme. Have students echo you as you sing the chant again. Then have students sing the chant as a group.

Distribute practice pages 56–58 and guide students in completing them.

Dictionary

 breakfast

 fiddlers

 jester

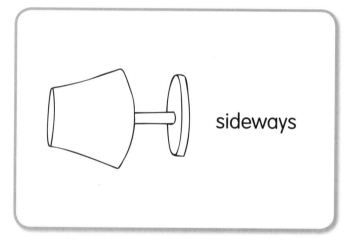 sideways

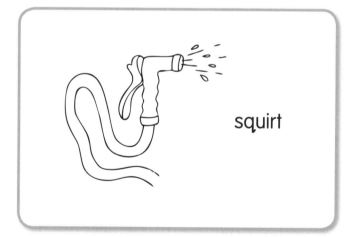 squirt

 yawning

Words to Know!

certainly	howled	imagine	instead
laugh	soul	suggest	swallow

Leveled Readers' Theater • EMC 3483 • © Evan-Moor Corp.

EMC 3483 • © Evan-Moor Corp.

Leveled Readers' Theater

Young King Cole

Written by: T. Heehee

_____
Name

EMC 3483 • © Evan-Moor Corp.

Leveled Readers' Theater

Storyteller: Old King Cole was a merry soul, but he hadn't always been that way. There was a time, when he was young, that King Cole didn't look so merry. The queen was very worried.

Queen: King Cole is no longer the happy prince I married. I miss seeing him smile. I miss hearing him laugh. He looks so unhappy these days. I must find out what's wrong.

1

Storyteller: That night after dinner, the king called for his fiddlers, but the queen came instead.

King: Oh, hello, dear. Have you seen the fiddlers?

2

Queen: I gave the fiddlers the night off. You and I have to talk.

King: Certainly, dear. What shall we talk about?

Queen: Tell me, Cole, are you unhappy?

King: My goodness, no. I can't imagine why you would ask me that.

3

EMC 3483 • © Evan-Moor Corp.

Leveled Readers' Theater

Queen: Well, you haven't laughed or smiled in more than a year.

King: Don't be silly. Of course I have! Why, just look at me. I'm smiling right now.

Queen: No. No you're not.

King: Well, I thought I was. But if you say I'm not, then it must be so. What can we do about it?

4

EMC 3483 • © Evan-Moor Corp.

Leveled Readers' Theater

Queen: Let's try a laugh. You used to laugh at my riddles, so here's one: What kind of shoes do frogs wear? Open toad. Ha, ha, ha, ha, ha … Get it? Open t-o-a-d … toad! Ha, ha, ha, ha, ha.

King: Yes, yes! I get it! My goodness, I'm laughing so hard, it hurts.

Queen: But you're not laughing! You're yawning.

5

King: I am? Oh! Well, I must be tired. Running a kingdom is a big job, you know. Now what shall we do?

Queen: We shall go to the jester's office first thing tomorrow morning. That's what we shall do.

Storyteller: And they did. When the king and queen got to the jester's office, the jester was just sitting down to breakfast.

6

Jester: What seems to be the problem?

Queen: King Cole does not laugh or smile anymore. You must help him.

Jester: Let me take a look. Okay, King Cole, open wide and say "HA!"

King: Heh … heh … heh … huh.

7

Jester: Hmm … yes. Very serious. I'm going to need some help. I will call in my team of fools.

Storyteller: Three fools named Chuckle, Cackle, and Snort tumbled into the jester's office.

Jester: King Cole smiles like a stone, and he has lost his laugh. We must help him. What do you fools suggest?

Cackle: Come closer, King. Now lean in and sniff the flower on my shirt. That's it. Take a real big sniff.

Storyteller: When King Cole was in the middle of a big sniff, Cackle made water squirt out of the flower, right into the king's face.

Cackle: I don't understand it. Everyone is laughing, except the king. Didn't you think my squirting flower was funny?

King: Yes! Yes! Very funny. I'm laughing my head off. Look! I'm even slapping my knee.

Jester: Hmm … laughing on the inside, nothing on the outside. The king's problem is much worse than I thought.

10

Chuckle: Let me take a crack at getting a smile. I know a very funny riddle.

Queen: I tried that yesterday.

Chuckle: But this one's really funny. Why did the banana go to the doctor? Give up? It wasn't peeling very well! Ha, ha, ha, ha, ha … hmpf! Still nothin'.

11

Snort: Allow me. Jester, may I borrow your banana? I'll need that glass of milk, too. Now, watch this!

Storyteller: Snort drank half the milk but didn't swallow it. Then he stuffed the banana into his mouth—sideways!

Snort: Ah…ah…ah…CHOO!

Storyteller: With a big banana grin on his face, Snort sneezed the milk out through his nose. Everyone howled with laughter, except, of course, the king.

12

Jester: We have teased and tickled. We've tried riddles and silly stunts. There's only one thing left to do.

Queen: What's that, Jester?

Jester: We must think about it.

Storyteller: The jester and the fools put their heads together. And they thought and they thought and they thought. Finally, they came up with the answer.

13

Jester: I think the problem, King Cole, is that you have been working too hard.

Cackle: You must take some time off…

Chuckle: …and go to Smile School.

Snort: Laughland has classes for adults.

King: But that's impossible! Who will take care of the kingdom?

Jester and Fools: We will!

Storyteller: When the king heard that, the corners of his mouth turned up, and a grin slowly spread across his chin. Suddenly, a big "HA!" burst out of his mouth. The thought of Jester and the fools taking care of the kingdom made the king laugh and laugh and laugh. And he's been a merry soul ever since.

Sing to the tune of
"I've Been Working on the Railroad."

Trying to Get a Smile

We've been trying to make the king smile
All the long, long year.
We've been trying to make the king smile
And show a little cheer.
We tried telling funny riddles.
All he did was sigh.
We've just got to make the king smile.
What else can we try?

We've been trying to make the king laugh
All the long, long year.
We've been trying to make the king laugh
And show a little cheer.
We played tricks and teased and tickled.
We even tried "Ah-Choo!"
We've just got to make the king laugh
If it's the last thing that we do.

Name _____

About the Play

Fill in the circle next to the correct answer.

1. What is the main problem in the play?

   Ⓐ The king is always having fun.
   Ⓑ The fiddlers will not play music.
   Ⓒ The king never laughs or smiles.

2. The queen took the king to visit _____.

   Ⓐ the fiddlers
   Ⓑ the jester
   Ⓒ the doctor

3. Who did the jester call for help?

   Ⓐ the fools
   Ⓑ the queen
   Ⓒ the fiddlers

4. What finally made the king laugh and smile?

   Ⓐ the jester's jokes
   Ⓑ the thought of the fools taking care of the kingdom
   Ⓒ the thought of the queen taking care of the kingdom

Leveled Readers' Theater • EMC 3483 • © Evan-Moor Corp.

Name _____

I Know the Words

Fill in the circle next to the correct answer.

1. If you **howled** with laughter, you laughed _____.

   Ⓐ very loudly   Ⓑ quietly   Ⓒ through your nose

2. The word **instead** means _____.

   Ⓐ wrong   Ⓑ the same   Ⓒ in place of

3. You **laugh** when you think something is _____.

   Ⓐ sad   Ⓑ funny   Ⓒ scary

4. You **swallow** after you _____.

   Ⓐ chew   Ⓑ bake   Ⓒ cut

5. You **yawn** when you are _____.

   Ⓐ happy   Ⓑ tired   Ⓒ sad

6. You eat **breakfast** in the _____.

   Ⓐ evening   Ⓑ afternoon   Ⓒ morning

Name _____

I Know What Happened

Look at each picture. Write sentences to tell what happened in the play.

1. _____

_____

_____

_____

_____

2. _____

_____

_____

_____

_____

3. _____

_____

_____

_____

_____

Home, Sweet Desert Home

This informational play introduces the many kinds of animals that live in a desert.

Characters

Chorus 1   Chorus 2   Chorus 3

---

1 **Build Background**

Ask students to share what they know about desert environments. Then ask students to name some of the animals that live in deserts.

2 **Assign Parts**

This play has reading parts for three choral groups. Each group reads its parts in unison. The readings are similar in repetition and general level of difficulty, and include content words such as **soar**, **slither**, **prowl**, and **stinging**. All of the reading parts are well suited to students reading on or below grade level.

3 **Introduce Vocabulary**

Dictionary: Point to each pictured word. Read the word aloud and have students echo you. Discuss word meaning as needed.

Words to Know: Point to each word. Read the word aloud and have students echo you. Remind students how to pronounce challenging phonetic structures. For the word **poison**, for example, you might say, *Remember, when the letters **oi** appear together in a word, they sound like /oy/.* Discuss word meaning as needed.

4 **Preview the Script**

Guide students in previewing the script. Have students look at the illustrations and make predictions about what will happen in the play. Then go through the script again, page by page, having students highlight their reading parts.

5 **Practice the Script and Share the Play**

Have students read the script aloud as a group several times. Model how to use intonation and expression to emphasize the rhyme. Then model how to use a hand signal as a cue for the members of a choral group to begin reading in unison. After students are able to read the script fluently, have them read the play for an audience.

6 **Conduct Follow-up Activities**

Model the chant for students. Talk about its rhythm and rhyme. Have students echo you as you sing the chant again. Then have students sing the chant as a group.

Distribute practice pages 70–72 and guide students in completing them.

Dictionary

 banded gecko

 bighorn sheep

 cactus wren

 red-tailed hawk

 roadrunner

 scorpion

 sidewinder

 stink beetle

Words to Know!

crawl	hooves	poison	prey
slither	soar	squirting	stinging

Leveled Readers' Theater • EMC 3483 • © Evan-Moor Corp.

EMC 3483 • © Evan-Moor Corp.

Leveled Readers' Theater

Home, Sweet Desert Home

Written by: Sonny Sands

_____
Name

Chorus 1: A desert seems to be just empty space.
Who would dare live in such a hot place?

Chorus 2: Animals that climb or crawl,
soar or slither, hop or prowl,
a desert seems to have them all!

2

Chorus 3: In a desert, you can spot
a brown bat, hanging around
a cactus and drinking from
its flowers …

3

Chorus 1: … and a red-tailed hawk,
hunting for food as it
soars on the wind.

4

Chorus 2: In a desert, you can spot a stink beetle,
standing on its head and squirting smelly stuff
to protect itself…

5

Chorus 3: …and a slithering sidewinder,
shaking the tip of its tail to
rattle a warning.

Chorus 1: In a desert, you can see bighorn sheep,
leaping from rock to rock, with hooves
that hold on tight …

Chorus 2: … and a little cactus wren,
kicking sand onto its feathers
to clean them.

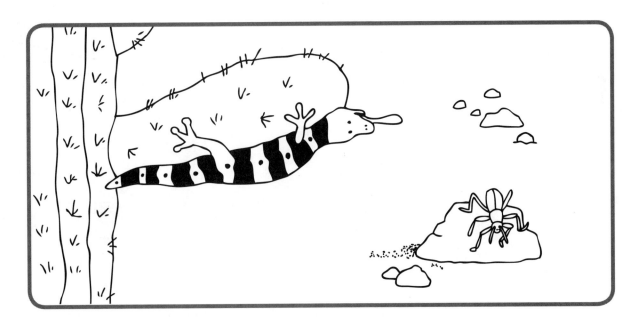

Chorus 3: In a desert, you can spot
a banded gecko, crawling
upside down and scooping
up bugs with its tongue …

EMC 3483 • © Evan-Moor Corp.

Chorus 1: . . . and a spotted bobcat,
napping before a
nighttime hunt.

EMC 3483 • © Evan-Moor Corp.

Chorus 2: In a desert, you can spot a
screech owl, listening for the
sound of food on the ground . . .

Chorus 3: … and a scary scorpion,
stinging its prey with poison.

Chorus 1: In a desert, you can see a kangaroo rat,
stuffing the seeds of grasses and weeds
into pouches in its cheeks…

Chorus 2: …and a roadrunner, racing a rat
to catch a meal with its beak.

Chorus 3: Animals that climb or crawl,
soar or slither, hop or prowl,
a desert seems to have them all!

Sing to the tune of
"Take Me Out to the Ball Game."

Take Me Out to the Desert

Take me out to the desert.
Take me out to the heat.
Show me some bighorns up on the rocks.
Show me roadrunners and red-tailed hawks.

Let me look, look, look for a gecko.
Can it really walk upside down?
It is fun to learn about creatures that call
   deserts their hometown.

Take me out to the desert.
Take me out to the sand.
Show me the brown bats and cactus wrens.
Show me this place where the sky never ends.

Let me search, search, search for a bobcat.
It has fur that's sprinkled with spots.
It is fun to learn about creatures that live
   where it's hot, hot, HOT!

Home, Sweet Desert Home 69

Name _____

About the Play

Fill in the circle next to the correct answer.

1. What does the play say about a desert?

  Ⓐ A desert is too hot for bugs.
  Ⓑ Many kinds of animals live in a desert.
  Ⓒ All deserts are the same.

2. Which are desert animals?

  Ⓐ bighorn sheep, brown bears, and lions
  Ⓑ spiders, owls, and horses
  Ⓒ banded geckos, brown bats, and bobcats

3. Which desert animal squirts smelly stuff to protect itself?

  Ⓐ sidewinder
  Ⓑ stink beetle
  Ⓒ banded gecko

4. A brown bat flies around a cactus to _____.

  Ⓐ drink from its flowers
  Ⓑ sleep on its flowers
  Ⓒ eat its flowers

Leveled Readers' Theater • EMC 3483 • © Evan-Moor Corp.

Name _____

I Know the Words

Fill in the circle next to the correct answer.

1. You **sting** prey if you are a _____.

   Ⓐ cactus wren   Ⓑ bobcat   Ⓒ scorpion

2. You have **hooves** if you are a _____.

   Ⓐ bighorn sheep   Ⓑ banded gecko   Ⓒ bobcat

3. You **slither** in the sand if you are a _____.

   Ⓐ hawk   Ⓑ sidewinder   Ⓒ bobcat

4. You **listen** for the sound of food if you are a _____.

   Ⓐ banded gecko   Ⓑ screech owl   Ⓒ scorpion

5. You **soar** as you hunt if you are a _____.

   Ⓐ red-tailed hawk   Ⓑ bighorn sheep   Ⓒ roadrunner

6. You **scoop** up bugs with your tongue if you are a _____.

   Ⓐ stink beetle   Ⓑ cactus wren   Ⓒ banded gecko

Name _____

I Know What Happened

Draw one desert animal in each box. Write about each animal on the lines.

1. _____

_____

_____

_____

_____

2. _____

_____

_____

_____

_____

3. _____

_____

_____

_____

_____

Why I Wear It

*This informational play is about a fictional animal fashion show
that features a special characteristic of each animal.*

Characters

Host	Leo	Freda	Marco	Calvin
Trevor	Olivia	Serena	Stella	

1 Build Background

Explain to students that animals
often develop physical features and
behaviors in order to adapt to their
environments. Then choose one
animal and invite students to help
you brainstorm its characteristics.

2 Assign Parts

All of the reading parts include
accessible content vocabulary, and
are well suited to students reading
on or above grade level.

3 Introduce Vocabulary

Dictionary: Point to each pictured
word. Read the word aloud and have
students echo you. Point out the
variant pronunciation of the letters **ch**
in the word **chameleon**. You might say,
for example, *When the letters **ch** appear
together at the beginning of a word, they
sometimes sound like /k/.* Another example
of this variant pronunciation is the word
character. Discuss word meaning
as needed.

Words to Know: Point to each word.
Read the word aloud and have students
echo you. Teach words with irregular
phonetic structures, such as **algae**,
fashion, and **disguise**, as sight words.
Discuss word meaning as needed.

4 Preview the Script

Guide students in previewing the
script. Have students look at the
illustrations and make predictions
about what will happen in the play.
Then go through the script again,
page by page, having students highlight
their reading parts.

**5 Practice the Script and
Share the Play**

Have students read the script aloud
as a group several times. Model how
to use intonation and expression to
develop each character's personality.
After students are able to read the script
fluently, have them read the play for
an audience.

6 Conduct Follow-up Activities

Model the chant for students. Talk
about its rhythm and rhyme. Have
students echo you as you recite the
chant again. Then have students recite
the chant as a group.

Distribute practice pages 84–86 and
guide students in completing them.

Dictionary

 chameleon

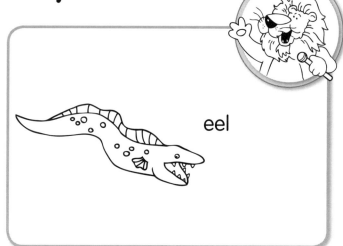 eel

 mane

 rainforest

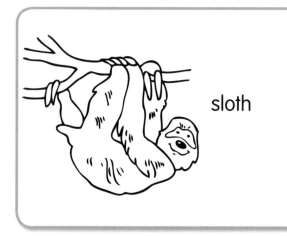 sloth

 toucan

Words to Know!

algae	Arctic	disguise	exactly	fashion
fierce	juicy	runway	stretch	unusual

Leveled Readers' Theater • EMC 3483 • © Evan-Moor Corp.

EMC 3483 • © Evan-Moor Corp.

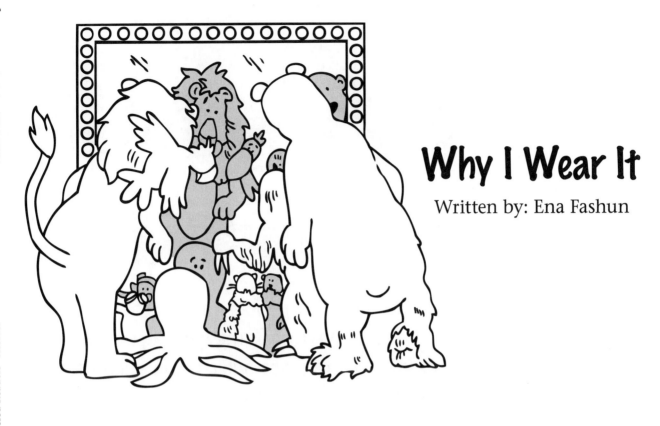

Why I Wear It

Written by: Ena Fashun

_____
Name

EMC 3483 • © Evan-Moor Corp.

Host: Good afternoon and welcome to the Animal Fashion Show. Let's give a warm welcome to the animals that are here today.
(All clap)

Host: Leo Lion, you look grand. Tell us about that fantastic fur piece you're wearing.

1

Leo: You must be talking about my thick, honey-gold mane. My mane makes me look big and fierce. It covers my throat, too, which makes it hard for another animal to grab me there.

2

Host: Now, here's Freda the flying squirrel. You look lovely, Freda. Is that a blanket you're wearing?

3

Freda: It looks like a blanket, but it's not. It's my skin. When I stretch out my front and back legs, the skin attached to them stretches, too. My skin spreads out like a blanket and helps me glide from tree to tree. It's not flying exactly, but it's a fast way to get away from big birds.

4

Host: Look at Marco Polar Bear! He's come all the way from the icy Arctic! That is a beautiful white fur coat, Marco!

5

Marco: Thanks. I need this coat to keep me warm and dry. It actually has two layers of fur. And the matching fur boots keep me from slipping and sliding on ice.

6

Host: Let's give a warm welcome to Calvin Chameleon. Hi, Cal! Nice shade of green you're wearing. Oh, I mean brown.

Calvin: These hot lights made my skin change from green to brown. My skin changes color when I'm hot and when I'm cold. It also changes color when I get angry. If I turn red and yellow—watch out!

7

Host: Well, look who flew in from the rainforest! It's Trevor Toucan. No wonder your huge beak has made you famous. It's bigger than your head!

8

Trevor: My beak is outstanding, isn't it? We toucans are the only birds with this type of beak. In fact, other birds and small animals do not even like to get near it. I find it very helpful, though. I use it like a long arm to pluck juicy berries off tree branches. It gives me quite a reach.

9

Host: Olivia Octopus, what is this I hear about
a black blob?

10

Olivia: Oh my, yes. The black blob. Well, that is my ink.
I use it as a disguise. When an eel tries to attack
me, I just squirt out some black ink. I turn myself
black, too. Then an eel can't tell the difference
between me and the black ink blob!

11

Host: Serena Sea Otter … fabulous as always.
I hear you have an unusual purse.

Serena: Yes, I do. It's one of a kind. It's a pouch of skin under
my front flipper, so I can't show you, of course.
But, I can tell you that I use it like a purse
to hold clams, crabs, and all the other things
a sea otter simply can't live without.

12

Host: We have saved the slowest animal for last. Here
comes Stella Sloth, inching down the runway. Tell us
about your coat, Stella. It's such an unusual color.

13

Stella: I live in a tropical rainforest, and this is my rainy-season coat. Usually, my coat is brown. But when it gets wet, tiny plants called algae live in it. The algae give me this mossy green color. I love it! When I'm hanging in a tree, which I do all the time, I am very hard to see.

14

Host: And so, that ends today's Animal Fashion Show. The next time you're checking out animal fashions, remember that the way an animal looks tells you a lot about where and how it lives. Until next time, stay in style!

15

Animals on the Runway

Roaring down the runway,
Leo Lion walks with pride.
His mane, all big and honey-gold,
Is swaying side to side.

Gliding down the runway,
Freda Squirrel is in a hurry.
With her skin stretched like a blanket,
She can "fly" instead of scurry.

Crawling down the runway,
Cal Chameleon wears green skin.
But when we see him near the lights,
Brown is what he's in.

Inching down the runway,
Stella Sloth makes quite a scene.
The algae in her brown fur
Make it look a mossy green.

Name _____

About the Play

Fill in the circle next to the correct answer.

1. What happens to a sloth's coat when it gets wet?

   Ⓐ It turns green.
   Ⓑ It gets sticky.
   Ⓒ It grows.

2. How do flying squirrels quickly get away from birds?

   Ⓐ They run fast.
   Ⓑ They glide from tree to tree.
   Ⓒ They jump from tree to tree.

3. Which animal flew to the fashion show?

   Ⓐ Leo Lion
   Ⓑ Stella Sloth
   Ⓒ Trevor Toucan

4. What color might a chameleon be when it is angry?

   Ⓐ green
   Ⓑ red
   Ⓒ purple

Name _____

I Know Who

Fill in the circle next to the animal that the clue describes.

1. My coat has two layers of fur.

   Ⓐ polar bear   Ⓑ lion   Ⓒ flying squirrel

2. Tiny plants called algae live in my wet fur.

   Ⓐ otter   Ⓑ sloth   Ⓒ lion

3. My skin changes colors.

   Ⓐ chameleon   Ⓑ octopus   Ⓒ sloth

4. My body squirts a blob of ink.

   Ⓐ lion   Ⓑ otter   Ⓒ octopus

5. I use my large beak to pick juicy berries from trees.

   Ⓐ sloth   Ⓑ chameleon   Ⓒ toucan

6. I have a pouch to hold my food.

   Ⓐ otter   Ⓑ octopus   Ⓒ chameleon

Writing Activity

Name _____

I Know What Happened

Look at each picture. Write sentences to tell about each animal's special characteristic.

1. _____

_____

_____

_____

_____

2. _____

_____

_____

_____

_____

3. _____

_____

_____

_____

_____

     Leveled Readers' Theater • EMC 3483 • © Evan-Moor Corp.

Come! Sit! Stay!

This play is about the grand opening of a dog training school, but from the dogs' points of view!

Characters

Narrator   Murphy   Pepper   Angel

Cocoa   Gonzo   Princess

---

1 Build Background

Explain that dogs have unique personalities just as people do. Ask students how many of them have dogs. Then ask each student to use one word to tell the class about his or her dog's personality. Tell students that this play is about six dogs, each with a different personality.

2 Assign Parts

The reading parts for the narrator are infrequent, but they are longer than the other reading parts, so they are well suited to a student reading on or above grade level. The reading parts for Murphy, Angel, Gonzo, and Princess are well suited to students reading on grade level. The reading parts for Pepper and Cocoa are short and repetitive, so they are well suited to students reading below grade level.

3 Introduce Vocabulary

Dictionary: Point to each pictured word. Read the word aloud and have students echo you. Discuss word meaning as needed.

Words to Know: Point to each word. Read the word aloud and have students echo you. Explain the use of slang to students, using **nuttin'** and **whadd'ya** as examples. Also point out the use of apostrophes to replace omitted letters. Discuss word meaning as needed.

4 Preview the Script

Guide students in previewing the script. Have students look at the illustrations and make predictions about what will happen in the play. Then go through the script again, page by page, having students highlight their reading parts.

5 Practice the Script and Share the Play

Have students read the script aloud as a group several times. Model how to use intonation and expression to develop each character's personality. After students are able to read the script fluently, have them read the play for an audience.

6 Conduct Follow-up Activities

Model the chant for students. Talk about its rhythm and rhyme. Have students echo you as you recite the chant again. Then have students recite the chant as a group.

Distribute practice pages 96–98 and guide students in completing them.

Dictionary

backflip

blocking

neighborhood

trainer

Words to Know!

advice	announces	behave	elegant	nuttin'
pardon	pleasant	ruckus	trampling	whadd'ya

EMC 3483 • © Evan-Moor Corp.

Leveled Readers' Theater

Come! Sit! Stay!

Written by: Kay Nines

_____
Name

EMC 3483 • © Evan-Moor Corp.

Leveled Readers' Theater

Narrator: Lately, Pleasant Street has been anything but pleasant. The neighborhood dogs have been running loose, trampling flowers, and chasing cats. Maybe that's why there's such a long line at Come! Sit! Stay! Dog Training School. It's the school's grand opening, and Murphy, Pepper, Angel, Cocoa, Gonzo, and Princess are all there.

1

Murphy: Come on, dogs. Line up! Let's show them that we already know how to behave.

Pepper: Where are we? What's going on? Do I smell food?

- -

Murphy: We're at school, Pepper.

Pepper: School? What school? What's a school?

Murphy: School is a place to learn things. We're here to learn how to behave.

Angel: If you really want to learn how to come, sit, and stay, all you have to do is watch me. I already know how to behave.

Cocoa: No! No! Watch me! Watch how high I can jump!

Gonzo: You call that a jump? I can do backflips higher than that!

Narrator: A black pug named Princess makes her way to the front of the line.

Princess: Pardon me. Move back, please. This is where I belong.

Angel: Princess, don't you know it's bad manners to cut in line?

4

Pepper: Line. What line? Am I in line?

Gonzo: Yeah, you're in line! Don't ya know nuttin'?

Cocoa: I know something! I know how to jump!

Murphy: Calm down, Cocoa! I told you we're here to learn to behave, not jump. And, Princess, you're going to have to go back to the end of the line.

Princess: I can't stand back there. A Great Dane is blocking the light. You can see how the light makes my black fur gleam.

Angel: This is dog training school, not a beauty contest.

5

Narrator: A trainer announces that class is ready to begin. The dogs make quite a ruckus as they enter the classroom. The trainer explains that, in the first lesson, each dog will learn to come when it hears its name.

Pepper: Name? Do I have a name? What's a name?

Gonzo: I know my name. They don't call me Gonzo the Growler for nuttin'. Grrrrrrr.

Angel: They call me Angel because I never do anything wrong.

Cocoa: I don't know why they call me Cocoa. All I know is I can really jump!

Murphy: They probably named you Cocoa beause you're brown. It looks like you fell into a pot of chocolate.

Princess: I'm sure I don't need to explain why they call me Princess. Just look at my elegant folds of fur and my jewel-like eyes. I look like royalty.

Gonzo: Aw, go on. You look like any other mutt.

Angel: Shh. Be quiet. The trainer is talking again. I think we're ready for the second lesson.

Pepper: Trainer? What trainer? What's a trainer?

Narrator: The trainer announces the second lesson. The dogs will learn how to sit.

Gonzo: Hey, whadd'ya know? There's only a few of us left for this sittin' thing. I guess most of the other mutts didn't even know their own names.

Cocoa: I don't want to sit! The next lesson should be how to jump! I love to jump!

8

Angel: If any of you want some advice on the best way to sit, just ask me. See? My back is straight, and I'm looking right at the trainer.

Gonzo: I don't need no advice. I'll sit how I wanna sit.

Princess: I just need to make sure I sit in the right light.

Murphy: We all have our own way of sitting. Let's listen up now. I think it's time for the next lesson.

9

Narrator: The Pleasant Street dogs were ready to show how well they could "stay" when the trainer announced that it was time to go.

Gonzo: That's it? That's all? That was nuttin'.

Angel: I think I did quite well.

Princess: I know I did well—very well.

Cocoa: I can do well! Watch me jump!

Murphy: Come on, dogs. Let's head home. It sounds like school is over for this week.

Pepper: School? What school? What's a school?
Hey! Where's everybody going?

My Dog's Day

How does my dog
Spend the day?
What does she do
When I'm away?

I paw and dig and
Carry a twig.
That's what's fun for me!

I bite and nip and
Chew and rip.
I feel so carefree!

I scamper and chase and
Pounce and race.
I'm on a playing spree!

I sleep and snore and
Lie on the floor and
Wish you'd come home to me.

Name _____

About the Play

Fill in the circle next to the correct answer.

1. What is the name of the dog training school?

   Ⓐ Come Here! Dog Training School
   Ⓑ Come! Sit! Stay! Dog Training School
   Ⓒ Behave! Dog Training School

2. Which dog seems to be the most playful?

   Ⓐ Angel
   Ⓑ Princess
   Ⓒ Cocoa

3. What was the dogs' first lesson?

   Ⓐ to jump high
   Ⓑ to sit
   Ⓒ to come when called by name

4. Which dog never knew what was going on at school?

   Ⓐ Angel
   Ⓑ Pepper
   Ⓒ Gonzo

Name _____

I Know the Words

Fill in the circle next to the correct answer.

1. If something is **pleasant**, it is _____.

   Ⓐ mean   Ⓑ sad   Ⓒ nice

2. If something is **elegant**, it is _____.

   Ⓐ fancy   Ⓑ dull   Ⓒ wet

3. If dogs are **trampling** flowers, they are _____.

   Ⓐ smelling them   Ⓑ walking on them   Ⓒ looking at them

4. If dogs are making a **ruckus**, they are _____.

   Ⓐ behaving   Ⓑ making noise   Ⓒ sleeping

5. The word **nuttin'** is slang for the word _____.

   Ⓐ nuts   Ⓑ nobody   Ⓒ nothing

6. The word **whadd'ya** is slang for the words _____.

   Ⓐ what do you   Ⓑ who are you   Ⓒ when did you

Name _____

I Know What Happened

Each dog at "Come! Sit! Stay! Dog Training School" has a different personality. Use the words in the box to complete the sentences.

advice	charge	energy	jump	leader	looks
lost	questions	royalty	rules	slang	tough

1. Cocoa has a lot of _____.

   He likes to _____ up and down.

2. Angel likes to follow the _____.

   She also likes to give _____.

3. Gonzo acts _____.

   He uses _____ when he speaks.

4. Princess pays a lot of attention to how she _____.

   She thinks she looks like _____.

5. Murphy likes to take _____.

   He is a good _____.

6. Pepper seems mixed-up or _____.

   He asks a lot of _____.

 Leveled Readers' Theater • EMC 3483 • © Evan-Moor Corp.

The Mystery at Coyote Cabin

This play is about three girls at summer camp who notice that items are mysteriously disappearing from their cabin.

Characters

Narrator   Holly   Hannah

Gwen   Greg   Matt

---

1 Build Background

Ask students to share what they know about summer camp. Discuss plants and animals that may live in and around a camp environment. Then discuss activities and traditions that might take place at an overnight summer camp. Invite students to share their experiences.

2 Assign Parts

The reading parts for the narrator are the most lengthy and are well suited to a student reading on or above grade level. The reading parts for the campers include content vocabulary, so they are also well suited to students reading on or above grade level.

3 Introduce Vocabulary

Dictionary: Point to each pictured word. Read the word aloud and have students echo you. Point out that several of the words are compound words. Discuss word meaning as needed.

Words to Know: Point to each word. Read the word aloud and have students echo you. Remind students how to pronounce the vowel digraphs in the words **counselors**, **roasting**, and **treasure**. Discuss word meaning as needed.

4 Preview the Script

Guide students in previewing the script. Have students look at the illustrations and make predictions about what will happen in the play. Then go through the script again, page by page, having students highlight their reading parts.

5 Practice the Script and Share the Play

Have students read the script aloud as a group several times. Model how to use intonation and expression to convey anger or confusion. After students are able to read the script fluently, have them read the play for an audience.

6 Conduct Follow-up Activities

Model the chant for students. Talk about its rhythm and rhyme. Have students echo you as you sing the chant again. Then have students sing the chant as a group.

Distribute practice pages 110–112 and guide students in completing them.

Dictionary

 campfire

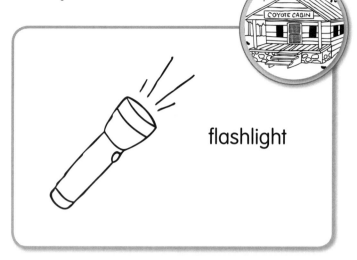 flashlight

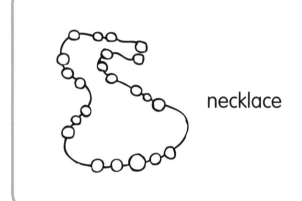 necklace

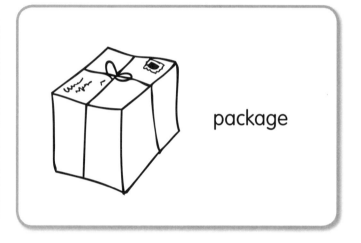 package

 pack rat

 wildflowers

Words to Know!

| accidentally | counselors | coyote | donated | knocked |
| occurred | pitch-dark | roasting | search | treasure |

Leveled Readers' Theater • EMC 3483 • © Evan-Moor Corp.

EMC 3483 • © Evan-Moor Corp.

Leveled Readers' Theater

The Mystery at Coyote Cabin

Written by: Wiley Rodent

_____

Name

Narrator: Gwen, Holly, and Hannah share Coyote Cabin. The three girls love being at summer camp. All day, they play games, go on hikes, and make crafts. At night, all the campers sit around a big campfire, roasting marshmallows, singing songs, and telling stories.

1

Holly: Come on, Hannah. If we don't get to the campfire soon, all the marshmallows will be gone.

Hannah: Just wait a minute. I'm looking for the necklace I made in crafts class yesterday. I want to wear it to the campfire. Have you seen it?

2

Holly: You mean the one with the red glass beads? I haven't seen it since you showed it to me yesterday. Maybe you left it in the bathroom.

Hannah: I'm sure I put it on the table next to my bed.

Gwen: Did you look on your bed?

Hannah: I looked on it, in it, and under it. My necklace is gone!

Gwen: Well, let's go to the campfire. Everyone will be there. We can ask if anyone has seen it.

3

Narrator: The next day, all the campers helped Hannah look for her necklace, but it never turned up. That night, another mystery occurred.

Holly: Look at my bed! It's wet! And the wildflowers I picked this morning are all over it. I had them in an old can on the shelf. Now the can is gone.

4

Hannah: Something weird is going on around here.

Gwen: Someone must have come in while we were at the campfire.

Holly: But wasn't everyone there with us?

Gwen: The boys from Vulture Cabin came late.

Holly: You mean Matt and Greg? You're right. They did show up late. And I'll just bet they know something about this.

Narrator: Holly, Gwen, and Hannah stormed over to Vulture Cabin.

5

Holly: You guys may think you're funny, but you're not. How would you like to sleep in a wet bed?

Greg: What are you talking about?

Holly: You know what I'm talking about! I had flowers in a can by my bed. Someone dumped the flowers and the water on my bed and took the can.

6

- -

Greg: Well, it wasn't us. We were at the campfire.

Gwen: But you were late! Where were you?

Matt: We had kitchen duty. Somebody probably knocked over the can accidentally and then threw it out.

Holly: Nobody should have been in our cabin in the first place. And you guys are always playing tricks.

Matt: We don't play dumb tricks like spilling water and stealing cans.

Greg: If you don't believe us, go ahead and search our cabin. See if you can find your old can.

7

EMC 3483 • © Evan-Moor Corp.

Gwen: Nobody could find anything in this cabin. Look at all the junk! Don't you ever clean up or throw anything away? It's like a pigpen in here!

EMC 3483 • © Evan-Moor Corp.

Narrator: The next day, Gwen got a package from home. It was a big batch of her mom's yummy oatmeal cookies. They were wrapped in shiny foil. Gwen decided to wait until after the camp talent show to eat them. When she returned, she couldn't believe her eyes.

Gwen: Oh no! Who spilled my cookies all over the place?

Hannah: Look, here's a piece of the foil they were wrapped in. Weird. Who would take the foil and leave the cookies?

Narrator: The girls could hardly sleep that night. Clouds covered the moon, so the cabin was pitch-dark. Around midnight, the girls heard *scratch… scratch… scratch…* It sent shivers up their spines.

Holly: What's that noise?

Hannah: I can't see a thing, and I can't find my flashlight.

Gwen: Well, I'm staying under the covers.

Narrator: In the morning, nothing seemed to be missing until Hannah went to put on her shoes.

Hannah: My shoelace is gone! Who would take one pink shoelace?

Gwen: I don't know. Just put on another pair of shoes. We have to hurry and eat breakfast so we don't miss the morning hike.

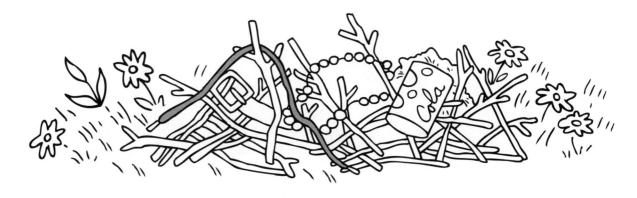

Narrator: After breakfast, the counselors led the campers on a hike through the woods. The sun was shining brightly as the campers looked at all the trees and flowers growing near the trail. One of the boys saw the sun reflect off something.

Matt: Hey! There's something shiny over there in that pile of twigs!

Narrator: The counselors explained that the pile of twigs was a pack rat's nest. The pack rat gathered the twigs and other things to make its home. The campers took a closer look.

Matt: Hey, I think I see some nails and a belt buckle in there. And some food wrappers! And you girls say our cabin looks like a pigpen?

Greg: Wow! Look over here. There's something red and shiny. Isn't that your necklace, Hannah?

EMC 3483 • © Evan-Moor Corp.

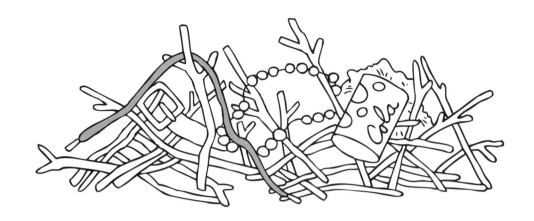

Hannah: It is! And there's my pink shoelace, too!

Greg: This little guy has a treasure chest in here!

Holly: I think that's the can my flowers were in!

14

- -

EMC 3483 • © Evan-Moor Corp.

Matt: This pack rat sure has a lot of stuff—and most of it's from Coyote Cabin! It looks like you girls donated the building supplies for a rodent's house.

Gwen: This rodent's house reminds me of your cabin! Maybe I should have called it a pack rat's nest instead of a pigpen!

15

Fun at Camp

We're at camp. We're at camp.
We're at camp, hip hip hooray!
We are having so much fun here
That we really want to stay.

Sleep in cabins. Sleep in cabins.
Sleep on damp and dusty beds.
Hear a lot of scary noises
And see spiders overhead.

Go out hiking. Go out hiking.
Every day, the sun is hot.
Got a million itchy bug bites.
Every night, we scratch a lot.

Eat s'mores. Eat s'mores.
Eat s'mores and want some more.
Marshmallows taste much better
When you're eating them outdoors.

We're at camp. We're at camp.
We're at camp, hip hip hooray!
We are having so much fun here
That we really want to stay.

Name _____

About the Play

Fill in the circle next to the correct answer.

1. What happened to the girls in Coyote Cabin?

   Ⓐ Someone or something was taking their things.
   Ⓑ Someone or something was cleaning their cabin.
   Ⓒ Someone or something was leaving them notes.

2. Who does Holly say is "always playing tricks"?

   Ⓐ the boys from Beaver Cabin
   Ⓑ the boys from Vulture Cabin
   Ⓒ the camp counselors

3. What did the campers see in the woods?

   Ⓐ a robin's nest
   Ⓑ a bear's cave
   Ⓒ a pack rat's nest

4. What did the pack rat use besides twigs to make its nest?

   Ⓐ leaves and eggshells
   Ⓑ foil, beads, a shoelace, and a can
   Ⓒ wildflowers, cookies, and string

   Leveled Readers' Theater • EMC 3483 • © Evan-Moor Corp.

Name _____

I Know the Words

Fill in the circle next to the correct answer.

1. If something **occurred**, it _____.

   Ⓐ happened   Ⓑ did not happen   Ⓒ might happen

2. If something is a **mystery**, it is _____.

   Ⓐ new   Ⓑ unexplained   Ⓒ known

3. If you are **roasting** something, you are _____.

   Ⓐ cooking it   Ⓑ making it   Ⓒ throwing it

4. If something is **pitch-dark**, it is _____.

   Ⓐ not dark   Ⓑ very dark   Ⓒ very light

5. When you **donate** something, you _____.

   Ⓐ buy it   Ⓑ sell it   Ⓒ give it away

6. What does it mean to **accidentally** do something?

   Ⓐ do it at night   Ⓑ do it by mistake   Ⓒ do it on purpose

Name _____

I Know What Happened

Use the words in the box to complete the story.

Cabin	crafts	foil	hike	necklace
nest	shiny	shoelace	Vulture	weird

Holly, Hannah, and Gwen shared Coyote _____ at summer

camp. They were having a fun time until _____ things

started happening. First, Hannah could not find the necklace she

made in _____ class. Later, Gwen's cookies were spilled

all over the place, and some of the _____ the cookies were

wrapped in was gone. Then, one of Hannah's shoes was missing

a _____.

The girls thought that the boys from _____ Cabin were

playing tricks on them, but during a _____ in the woods,

Matt saw something _____ in a pile of twigs. The twigs were

a pack rat's _____. A pack rat had gone into Coyote Cabin

and had taken the _____, the foil, and the shoelace!

 Leveled Readers' Theater • EMC 3483 • © Evan-Moor Corp.

Quangle Wangle Quee

This rhyming play uses fantasy characters and nonsense words to tell the story of the Quangle Wangle's remarkable hat.

 **Characters**

Quangle Wangle   Reader 1   Reader 2

Reader 3   Chorus

---

1 Build Background

Explain to students that nonsense rhyme uses invented language and fantasy characters, such as the Quangle Wangle Quee, to entertain. Tell students that part of the fun of reading nonsense rhyme is using their imaginations to picture the characters and what the characters are doing.

2 Assign Parts

This play has reading parts for at least six students. Because of all the nonsense words, most of which have unknown meanings, and the rich and unusual language, this play is well suited to students reading above grade level.

3 Introduce Vocabulary

Nonsense Dictionary: Point to each word. Read the word aloud and have students echo you. Remind students that these are nonsense words used to describe silly characters and objects. Either before or after reading the play, have students use their imaginations to draw a picture next to each nonsense word.

Words to Know: Point to each word. Read the word aloud and have students echo you. Discuss word meaning as needed.

4 Preview the Script

Guide students in previewing the script. Have students look at the illustrations and make predictions about what will happen in the play. Then go through the script again, page by page, having students highlight their reading parts.

5 Practice the Script and Share the Play

Have students read the script aloud as a group several times. Model how to use intonation and expression to emphasize rhythm and rhyme. After students are able to read the script fluently, have them read the play for an audience.

6 Conduct Follow-up Activities

Model the chant for students. Talk about its rhythm and rhyme. Emphasize the vowel sound featured in each verse. Have students echo you as you recite the chant again. Then have students recite the chant as a group.

Distribute practice pages 122–124 and guide students in completing them.

Nonsense Dictionary

Use your imagination to draw a picture next to each word or words.

Attery Squash	bibbons
Bisky Bat	Dong
Fimble Fowl	Olympian Bear
Orient Calf	Pobble

Words to Know!

account	airy	broad	corkscrew
Crumpetty Tree	luminous	plainer	Quangle Wangle Quee

                                    Leveled Readers' Theater • EMC 3483 • © Evan-Moor Corp.

Leveled Readers' Theater

Quangle Wangle Quee

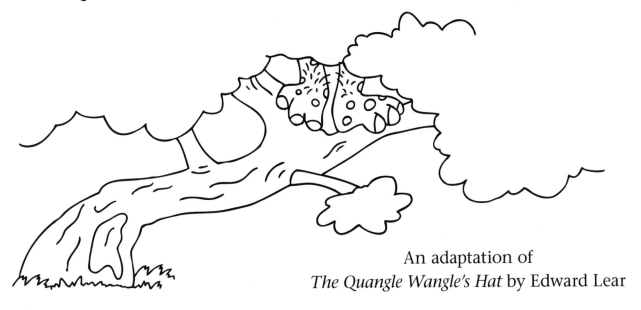

An adaptation of
The Quangle Wangle's Hat by Edward Lear

_____
Name

Leveled Readers' Theater

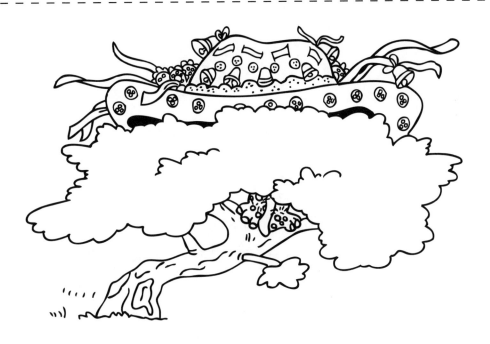

Reader 1: On the top of the Crumpetty Tree,
The Quangle Wangle sat,
But his face you could not see
On account of his lovely hat.

Quangle Wangle: My hat is a hundred and two feet wide,
With ribbons and bibbons on every side,
And bells and buttons and loops and lace,
So that nobody ever will see the face
Of the Quangle Wangle Quee.

2

Reader 2: The Quangle Wangle said to himself,
As he sat on the Crumpetty Tree—

Quangle Wangle: Jam and jelly and bread
Are the best of foods for me!
But the longer I live on the Crumpetty Tree,
The plainer than ever it seems to me
That very few people come this way,
And that life on the whole is far from gay!

3

Reader 3: But there came to the Crumpetty Tree,
Tweet dee dee, tweet dee dee,
Mr. and Mrs. Canary.

4

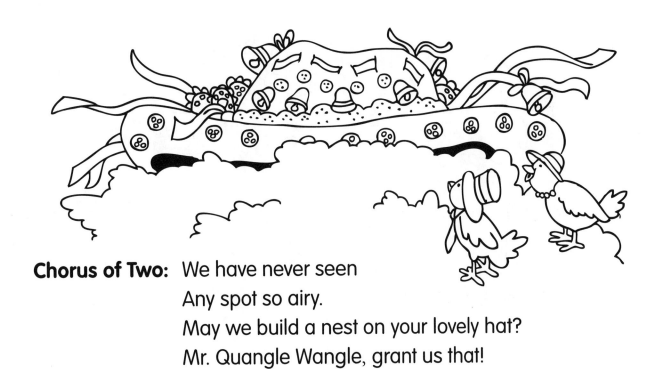

Chorus of Two: We have never seen
Any spot so airy.
May we build a nest on your lovely hat?
Mr. Quangle Wangle, grant us that!
Oh, please, let us come and build a nest
Of whatever material suits you best,
Mr. Quangle Wangle Quee!

5

Reader 1: And besides, to the Crumpetty Tree,
Came a stork, a duck, and an owl;
A snail and a bumblebee;

Reader 2: A frog and a Fimble Fowl,
(The Fimble Fowl had a corkscrew leg)
And all of them said—

Chorus: We humbly beg,
May we build our homes on your lovely hat?
Mr. Quangle Wangle, grant us that,
Mr. Quangle Wangle Quee.

Reader 3: And a Golden Grouse came there,
And a Pobble who has no toes
And a furry Olympian Bear
And a Dong with a luminous nose—

8

Reader 1: And a blue baboon who played the flute
And an Orient Calf from the Land of Tute
And an Attery Squash and a Bisky Bat—

9

Reader 2:   All came and built homes on the lovely hat
Of the Quangle Wangle Quee.
And the Quangle Wangle said to himself,
As he sat on the Crumpetty Tree—

Quangle Wangle: When all these creatures move,
What a wonderful noise there'll be!

Chorus: And at night, by the light of the Mulberry Moon,
They danced to the flute of the blue baboon
On the broad green leaves of the Crumpetty Tree,
And all were as happy as happy could be
With the Quangle Wangle Quee.

Chant

Follow the rhythm and rhyme, emphasizing vowel sounds, to recite this chant.

Quangle Wangle

Quangle Wangle Quee!
Quangle Wangle Quee!
How happy it makes me
To be a Quangle Wangle Quee!

Quangle Wangle Quoe!
Quangle Wangle Quoe!
How do you know
If you're a Quangle Wangle Quoe?

Quangle Wangle Quay!
Quangle Wangle Quay!
It's such fun to play
When you're a Quangle Wangle Quay!

Quangle Wangle Quoo!
Quangle Wangle Quoo!
Who, who, who
Is a Quangle Wangle Quoo?

Name _____

About the Play

Fill in the circle next to the correct answer.

1. Where is the Quangle Wangle Quee?

   Ⓐ in a house
   Ⓑ in the Crumpetty Tree
   Ⓒ in an oak tree

2. Why can't anyone see the Quangle Wangle's face?

   Ⓐ He wears a big hat.
   Ⓑ His hair is too long.
   Ⓒ He doesn't have a face.

3. What is the best food for the Quangle Wangle Quee?

   Ⓐ butter and jelly
   Ⓑ jam and eggs
   Ⓒ jam, jelly, and bread

4. What did the animals want to build on the Quangle Wangle's hat?

   Ⓐ their homes
   Ⓑ a barn
   Ⓒ tables and chairs

5. What sound did all the animals dance to?

   Ⓐ the screeching of a Bisky Bat
   Ⓑ the flute of the blue baboon
   Ⓒ the chirping of Mr. and Mrs. Canary

Name _____

I Know the Words

Fill in the circle next to the correct answer.

1. If a place is **airy**, it has _____.

   Ⓐ no space   Ⓑ a lot of space   Ⓒ very little space

2. The word **luminous** means _____.

   Ⓐ noisy   Ⓑ small   Ⓒ shining

3. The phrase **on account of** means _____.

   Ⓐ instead of   Ⓑ because of   Ⓒ besides

4. The word **creatures** is another word for _____.

   Ⓐ hats   Ⓑ trees   Ⓒ animals

5. The word **plain** means _____.

   Ⓐ ordinary   Ⓑ busy   Ⓒ loud

Name _____

I Know What Happened

Look at each picture. Write sentences to tell what happened in the play.

1. _____

_____

_____

_____

_____

2. _____

_____

_____

_____

_____

3. _____

_____

_____

_____

_____

Going Green

Level M

This play is about a girl who helps her family live a more eco-friendly lifestyle.

Characters

Gavin   Mom   Gloria   Narrator

1 Build Background

Explain to students that people use the term "green" to describe products and actions that prevent damage to the environment. Provide an example of how your school is "going green." Then ask students to share examples of how they are "going green" at home.

2 Assign Parts

The reading parts for the narrator and Gloria include content vocabulary words such as **environmentally**, **preservatives**, and **resources**, so they are well suited to students reading above grade level. The reading parts for Gavin and Mom are well suited to students reading on grade level.

3 Introduce Vocabulary

Words to Know: Point to each word. Read the word aloud and have students echo you. Support students with strategies for reading multisyllabic words. You might, for example, model how to underline parts of words to make longer words more accessible. Discuss word meaning as needed.

4 Preview the Script

Guide students in previewing the script. Have students look at the illustrations and make predictions about what will happen in the play. Then go through the script again, page by page, having students highlight their reading parts.

5 Practice the Script and Share the Play

Have students read the script aloud as a group several times. Model how to use intonation and expression to speak persuasively. After students are able to read the script fluently, have them read the play for an audience.

6 Conduct Follow-up Activities

Model the chant for students. Talk about its rhythm and rhyme. Have students echo you as you recite the chant again. Then have students recite the chant as a group.

Distribute practice pages 136–138 and guide students in completing them.

Words to Know

additives

homemade

cardboard

ingredients

conserving

packaging

definitely

pollute

disgusting

preservatives

eco-friendly

reusable

environmentally

reuse

exhaust

swallowed

Leveled Readers' Theater • EMC 3483 • © Evan-Moor Corp.

Going Green

Written by: Dave N. Urgie

_____
Name

Gavin: Ever since my sister Gloria came home from summer camp, all we ever hear about is conserving energy and saving Mother Earth. She doesn't even want me to eat my favorite corn chips anymore because the bag is not "eco-friendly." She has our house "going green," and I'm going crazy!

Mom: I'm going to the grocery store, kids.
We need a few things.

Gloria: Remember, Mom, only buy things that
are eco-friendly. Are you driving to the store?

2

Mom: I was planning to.

Gloria: Mom, the grocery store is only a short bike
ride away. There's no need to pollute the air
with car exhaust.

Mom: Would you like to ride your bike to the grocery
store and do the shopping?

Gloria: Sure!

Gavin: Don't forget to buy corn chips, Gloria!
I'll reuse the bag!

3

Narrator: Gloria attached a wicker basket to the front of her bike and a larger metal basket to the back of it. She grabbed two of the canvas tote bags she made at camp and headed for the store. When she got there, it didn't take her long to review the shopping list and decide which items were healthy and eco-friendly and which items weren't.

4

Gloria: Frozen peas, chocolate cookies, frozen burritos. All of this stuff has additives, preservatives, and worst of all—plastic packaging!

Narrator: By the time Gloria rode home, both of the canvas bags and the wicker basket were full of fresh fruits, vegetables, and ingredients for several recipes.

5

Gloria: Mom and Gavin are going to be so surprised when they see how much better it is to eat snacks and meals made with fresh ingredients. And we won't be wasting Earth's resources by using plastic and cardboard packaging.

Narrator: Gloria made a quick stop at the dollar store and then rode home.

Mom: That was fast, Gloria. But this looks like a lot more than what I had on the list.

Gavin: It's a lot of junk! Whole-wheat flour, vegetables, carob chips. Where are the chocolate cookies?

6

Mom: That's enough, Gavin. Did you forget to buy bottled water, Gloria?

Gloria: Nope, I didn't forget. Plastic water bottles are not environmentally friendly, Mom. I picked up three reusable water bottles at the dollar store.

Gavin: Okay, now she's outta' control, Mom!

7

Mom: So we can just refill these bottles here at home? You're already saving me money! This "going green" isn't a bad idea.

Gloria: I know, and I even bought ingredients to make homemade cookies and burritos.

Gavin: That's it! First my chips and now my cookies? You've gone too far!

8

Gloria: Calm down, Gavin. I'll make cookies for you.

Mom: Do you know how to make cookies?

Gloria: Sure, they taught me how to make eco-friendly meals at camp. In fact, I'll make dinner and dessert tonight.

Gavin: I'm eating out. I'm definitely eating out!

9

Narrator: Gloria opened her eco-friendly recipe book and started making cookies. She mixed whole-wheat flour, eggs, sugar, honey, and her secret ingredient—bananas! Then she poured in loads of carob chips and put the cookies in the oven to bake. A short time later, Gavin came into the kitchen.

10

Gavin: What's that smell?

Gloria: Hmm? What smell?

Gavin: You know what smell, Gloria! What are you making?

Gloria: I'm making eco-friendly, healthy cookies.

Gavin: They sound disgusting.

11

Gloria: Really? Well, they're ready to come out of the oven, and I happen to know that they are delicious. But since you don't want anything that's "disgusting," I guess you won't be having any.

Mom: What is that amazing smell? Cookies … ooh … and they're warm! Oh, Gloria, these are, oh … yum!

Narrator: While Gavin didn't think anyone was looking, he took a cookie off the plate, smelled it, and popped the whole thing into his mouth.

12

Mom: What do you think, Gavin?

Gavin: Ug, hmp, umf … about?

Gloria: Gavin! Your mouth is full of cookies, isn't it?

Narrator: Gavin took two more cookies, popped them into his mouth, and quickly chewed and swallowed them.

Gavin: Not anymore!

13

Gloria: I knew this family would like going green. I'd better start boiling the black beans. They're still in the canvas bag.

Mom: Are you making homemade burritos for dinner?

Gloria: Yep. Homemade and eco-friendly. No cardboard, no plastic, and no preservatives.

Gavin: They sound …

Gloria: What?

Gavin: Actually, if they're half as good as these cookies, they sound delicious. Now let's discuss homemade, eco-friendly corn chips!

Our Friend Earth

G-R-E-E-N
G-R-E-E-N
G-R-E-E-N
Planet Earth is our friend.

Reduce, reuse, recycle.
That's all you need to do.
Be a friend to Earth,
And Earth will be a friend to you.

G-R-E-E-N
G-R-E-E-N
G-R-E-E-N
Planet Earth is our friend.

Reduce!
Reuse!
Recycle!

Name _____

About the Play

Fill in the circle next to the correct answer.

1. Where did Gloria learn about "going green"?

   Ⓐ at school
   Ⓑ at summer camp
   Ⓒ at her friend's house

2. What did Gloria buy at the dollar store?

   Ⓐ candy
   Ⓑ paper bags
   Ⓒ reusable water bottles

3. What did Gloria make for Gavin?

   Ⓐ cookies
   Ⓑ vegetables
   Ⓒ corn chips

4. Why was the food Gloria cooked "eco-friendly"?

   Ⓐ It was from her garden.
   Ⓑ It was homemade and had no cardboard or plastic packaging.
   Ⓒ It was green in color.

                                    Leveled Readers' Theater • EMC 3483 • © Evan-Moor Corp.

Name _____

I Know the Words

Fill in the circle next to the correct answer.

1. The word **reuse** means to _____.

   Ⓐ use again   Ⓑ eat quickly   Ⓒ not use again

2. The word **eco-friendly** means _____.

   Ⓐ bad for Earth   Ⓑ good for Earth   Ⓒ made from earth

3. The word **definitely** means _____.

   Ⓐ maybe   Ⓑ for sure   Ⓒ probably

4. The word **conserving** means _____.

   Ⓐ wasting   Ⓑ using up   Ⓒ using carefully

5. The word **disgusting** means _____.

   Ⓐ yucky   Ⓑ yummy   Ⓒ young

Name _____

I Know What Happened

Look at each picture. Write sentences to tell what happened in the play.

1. _____

_____

_____

_____

_____

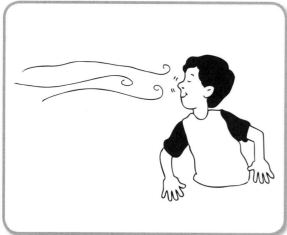

2. _____

_____

_____

_____

_____

3. _____

_____

_____

_____

_____

The Lost Half-Hour

This folk tale-style play is about a boy who helps people find what they have lost.

Characters

Storyteller	Arnold	Henry	Angry Man
Tall Man	Father Time	Chorus	

---

1 Build Background

Explain to students that this play uses idioms. Write the following two idioms on the board: "We all need to stick together." "He lost his temper." Then explain that an idiom is a group of words or a phrase that has developed a special meaning. Discuss the idioms you wrote on the board and invite students to share their ideas about what each idiom means.

2 Assign Parts

The storyteller's reading parts are frequent and lengthy, so they are well suited to a student reading on or above grade level. The reading parts for Angry Man and Tall Man are also well suited to students reading on or above grade level. The reading parts for Arnold, Henry, and Father Time are short and simple, so they are well suited to students reading on or below grade level. Most of the reading parts for the chorus include rhyme, so they are also well suited to students reading on or below grade level.

3 Introduce Vocabulary

Point to each word on the dictionary page. Read the word aloud and have students echo you. Have students look up each word in a dictionary and write its definition on the lines provided.

Remind students to look for the definition that reflects the way the word is used in the context of the play. The word **yowl**, for example, can be either a noun or a verb, but it is used as a noun in the play. Discuss definitions and usage as needed.

4 Preview the Script

Guide students in previewing the script. Have students look at the illustrations and make predictions about what will happen in the play. Then go through the script again, page by page, having students highlight their reading parts.

5 Practice the Script and Share the Play

Have students read the script aloud as a group several times. Model how to use intonation and expression to develop each character's personality. After students are able to read the script fluently, have them read the play for an audience.

6 Conduct Follow-up Activities

Model the chant for students. Talk about its rhythm and rhyme. Have students echo you as you recite the chant again. Then have students recite the chant as a group.

Distribute practice pages 152–154 and guide students in completing them.

Level N

Dictionary

Read each word. Write the definition on the lines.

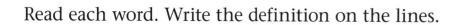

astray: _____

_____

_____

clockmaker: _____

_____

_____

countryside: _____

_____

_____

explode: _____

_____

_____

firecrackers: _____

_____

_____

grandfather clock: _____

_____

_____

jousting: _____

_____

_____

motioned: _____

_____

_____

nerve: _____

_____

_____

quiver: _____

_____

_____

slay: _____

_____

_____

yowl: _____

_____

_____

     Leveled Readers' Theater • EMC 3483 • © Evan-Moor Corp.

The Lost Half-Hour

Written by: Playon Words

EMC 3483 • © Evan-Moor Corp.

Leveled Readers' Theater

_____
Name

EMC 3483 • © Evan-Moor Corp.

Leveled Readers' Theater

Storyteller: Once upon a time, there was an old clockmaker. His name was Arnold Hinds. Arnold was a busy man. He was busy all the time.

Arnold: Look at the time! Another day is done, and I have not finished the clocks. How is it that I always have so many clocks but never enough time?

1

Storyteller: Arnold had a son named Henry. Henry liked to help his father in the clock shop. He swept the floor, dusted shelves, and ran errands. He also helped his father find things around the shop.

Arnold: Oil … oil … where is the oil? Henry, have you seen the oil?

Henry: Don't worry, Father. I will find it for you.

Storyteller: The clockmaker was always losing things, and he always asked Henry to find them.

Chorus: He asked Henry to find his tools, his eyeglasses, and his socks. Sometimes, he even asked Henry to find one of the clocks!

Storyteller: No matter what Arnold lost, Henry always found it. One morning, Arnold and Henry went to the clock shop later than usual. They had stayed in bed too long. Arnold had forgotten to wind the alarm clock.

Arnold: Henry! Henry! What shall I do? Mrs. Miller wants her clock by two! I cannot finish it in time. I've lost a half-hour this morning.

Henry: Don't worry, Father. I will find it for you.

Chorus: Henry looked in the shop. The half-hour wasn't there. So he dashed down the street. There was no time to spare.

Storyteller: Henry asked people if they had seen the lost half-hour, but no one had. So he hopped onto his horse and rode through the countryside.

Chorus: Henry rode on for hours. And then, for a minute, he stopped near a tree with an owl's nest in it.

Henry: Where has the time gone? A lost half-hour is certainly a hard thing to find.

Chorus: The owl heard Henry. The owl was wise. He hooted to Henry. Don't you know? Time flies!

6

Henry: Then I must not lose another second!

Storyteller: Henry rode through the countryside and then up a steep hill. At the top, he met a man whose hair stuck out like firecrackers. The man seemed ready to explode.

Henry: Tell me, sir, have you seen a lost half-hour?

7

EMC 3483 • © Evan-Moor Corp.

Angry Man: No! I'm looking for something much more important. I lost my temper two years ago, and I still haven't found it. Have you seen my lost temper? It is big and black and has spikes sticking out of it.

Henry: I haven't seen anything like that, but I am very good at finding things. Don't worry. I will find it for you.

Angry Man: Why do you want to find it for me? I'd better make sure you don't run off with it. I'm coming with you.

EMC 3483 • © Evan-Moor Corp.

Chorus: And so, down the hill they went, back to the countryside. Neither time nor temper did Henry find, although he really tried.

Angry Man: Now what? The road has ended at a thick forest. We will never find anything in there.

Henry: I must find my father's lost half-hour! I will tie my horse to a tree and look for a path.

Tall Man: Once you go in, you will never come out.

Angry Man: Who's there? Who said that?

Chorus: A tall man stepped out from behind a wide tree. He wore a metal suit. His eyes were all you could see.

Tall Man: Who are you? And why are you here?

10

- -

Henry: I am Henry Hinds. I am trying to find the half-hour my father lost this morning.

Angry Man: He is trying to find my temper, too! Now tell us, tall man, who are you?

Tall Man: I am no one … anymore. I was a brave and noble knight, until I lost a jousting fight. Now I hide at the edge of the wood. I've lost my nerve. It's gone for good.

Henry: One fight, good knight? Your nerve is not lost—just gone astray! We'll find your courage— perhaps today!

11

Angry Man: Wait a minute! Me first! What about my temper? Have you forgotten about my temper?

Storyteller: Henry motioned for both men to follow him down a winding path. The tall man stayed close beside him. The angry man grumbled along behind them.

Chorus: Deep in the forest, the group of three came upon an unusual tree. The tree had hands upon its face and, in its trunk, was a cupboard space.

12

Henry: Pardon me, Mr. Tree.

Father Time: First of all, I'm not a tree. I'm a grandfather clock. Did you look at me?

Henry: Actually, I was looking for a half-hour. Have you seen one go by?

13

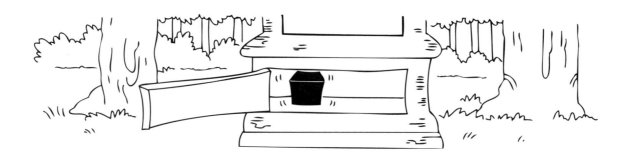

Father Time: A half-hour goes by every thirty minutes. When the next one comes along, I will warn you with a BONG!

Angry Man: What about me? Have you seen my lost temper?

Father Time: Yes. Open the door below my face. There's a black box in my cupboard space. Until you know the time is right, keep the box closed very tight.

14

Angry Man: How will I know when the time is right?

Father Time: The time is right when you have to fight. As for you, Henry—*tick … tick … tick …* BONG! There's your half-hour! Go now! Don't waste time!

Storyteller: Henry ran down the path as fast as he could. Angry Man and Tall Man ran after him. Suddenly, Henry stopped. A sleeping dragon was blocking the path.

15

Henry: Oh no! I must get by this dragon, or I'll never get back to the shop in time.

Chorus: Angry Man hoped to help Henry somehow. Then, remembering what the clock said, he let out a yowl!

Angry Man: The time is right! It's time to fight!

Storyteller: He gave Tall Man the box, still shut very tight.

Tall Man: I will use the temper you've been keeping to slay the dragon while it's sleeping!

Storyteller: Tall Man boldly walked up to the dragon and placed the box under its nose. Within an instant, smoke arose. The box began to quiver and shake, and then—BOOM!

Chorus: The black box blew up with a booming sound, and then dragon scales drifted to the ground.

Storyteller: The angry man smiled. The knight stood tall. Both had found what they needed after all.

Chorus: Henry Hinds lost no more time. He rushed back home. So ends this rhyme.

So Much to Lose!

Did you ever lose your temper?
Didn't keep it stuffed inside?
Did it burst out loud like thunder,
Then you wished that you could hide?

Did you ever lose a tooth?
Did it go without a trace?
One day, it started wiggling,
And now there's just a space?

Did you ever want to do something
You lost the chance to do?
Did you miss a night of trick-or-treat
Because you had the flu?

Did you ever lose a pound
And then wonder where it was?
Did it float out into space
As a gigantic ball of fuzz?

You have so much to lose.
You could even lose your mind!
So just keep an eye on everything,
Then you'll have much less to find.

Name _____

About the Play

Fill in the circle next to the correct answer.

1. Henry Hinds was good at _____.

   Ⓐ cooking food
   Ⓑ finding things
   Ⓒ jousting

2. Why did Angry Man smile?

   Ⓐ He smiled because he had used his temper to help Henry.
   Ⓑ He smiled because he had found his temper.
   Ⓒ He smiled because he found Father Time.

3. What did Tall Man do that showed he had found his nerve?

   Ⓐ He followed Henry and Angry Man into the forest.
   Ⓑ He talked to Father Time.
   Ⓒ He boldly placed a box under a dragon's nose.

4. What was Henry riding through the countryside looking for first?

   Ⓐ his father's lost half-hour
   Ⓑ Tall Man's lost nerve
   Ⓒ Angry Man's lost temper

Name _____

I Know the Words

Fill in the circle next to the correct answer.

1. To have **nerve** means to have _____.

   Ⓐ fear   Ⓑ courage   Ⓒ a metal suit

2. To **quiver** means to _____.

   Ⓐ jump   Ⓑ sleep   Ⓒ shake

3. To **drift** means to _____.

   Ⓐ sit still   Ⓑ roll in the dirt   Ⓒ be carried along by air

4. To **explode** means to _____.

   Ⓐ hide   Ⓑ blow up   Ⓒ ride a horse

5. When you lose your **temper**, you are _____.

   Ⓐ scared   Ⓑ angry   Ⓒ happy

6. What would you see in the **countryside**?

   Ⓐ hills and trees   Ⓑ many houses   Ⓒ tall buildings

Comprehension Activity

Name _____

I Know What Happened

Look at each picture. Write sentences to tell what happened in the play.

1. _____

_____

_____

_____

_____

2. _____

_____

_____

_____

_____

3. _____

_____

_____

_____

_____

Leveled Readers' Theater • EMC 3483 • © Evan-Moor Corp.

Answer Key

Page 16

Comprehension Activity

Name _____

About the Play

Fill in the circle next to the correct answer.

1. The play uses the names of states _____
   - Ⓐ to explain where they are
   - ● in funny puns that rhyme
   - Ⓒ in alphabetical order

2. What is Harry's quota of ice-cream sundaes?
   - ● three
   - Ⓑ four
   - Ⓒ five

3. Which words tell about the boy named Ill?
   - Ⓐ quiet, shy
   - ● a pest, bothersome
   - Ⓒ sad, upset

4. Why did Jason buy a new football jersey?
   - Ⓐ He ate too many ice-cream sundaes.
   - Ⓑ He joined a new team.
   - ● He ate too many pizzas.

16   Silly States   Leveled Readers' Theater • EMC 3483 • © Evan-Moor Corp.

Page 17

Vocabulary Activity

Name _____

I Know the Words

Fill in the circle next to the correct answer.

1. What does a **steed** need?
   - Ⓐ gas   Ⓑ oil   ● exercise

2. What is at the **shore**?
   - Ⓐ books   ● sand   Ⓒ corn

3. What do you do with a **sundae**?
   - Ⓐ sail it   Ⓑ water-ski in it   ● eat it

4. What do you do when you are **thirsty**?
   - ● drink something   Ⓑ go shopping   Ⓒ brush your teeth

5. What does a **pest** do?
   - ● bothers people   Ⓑ sells books   Ⓒ water-skis

6. What is a **nickname**?
   - Ⓐ a pet   Ⓑ a vacation   ● a shortened name

© Evan-Moor Corp. • EMC 3483 • Leveled Readers' Theater   Silly States   17

Page 18

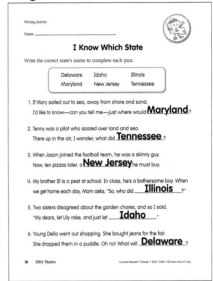

Writing Activity

Name _____

I Know Which State

Write the correct state's name to complete each pun.

| Delaware | Idaho | Illinois |
| Maryland | New Jersey | Tennessee |

1. If Mary sailed out to sea, away from shore and sand,
   I'd like to know—can you tell me—just where would **Maryland**?

2. Tenny was a pilot who soared over land and sea.
   There up in the air, I wonder, what did **Tennessee**?

3. When Jason joined the football team, he was a skinny guy.
   Now, ten pizzas later, a **New Jersey** he must buy.

4. My brother Ill is a pest at school. In class, he's a bothersome boy. When
   we get home each day, Mom asks, "So, who did **Illinois**?"

5. Two sisters disagreed about the garden chores, and so I said,
   "My dears, let Lily rake, and just let **Idaho**."

6. Young Della went out shopping. She bought jeans for the fair.
   She dropped them in a puddle. Oh no! What will **Delaware**?

18   Silly States   Leveled Readers' Theater • EMC 3483 • © Evan-Moor Corp.

Page 28

Comprehension Activity

Name _____

About the Play

Fill in the circle next to the correct answer.

1. Why is Evan stuck "in the middle"?
   - Ⓐ His little sister gets into trouble.
   - Ⓑ He doesn't have his own room.
   - ● He isn't the oldest, and he isn't the youngest.

2. What does Dillon want to do before he helps watch Emma?
   - ● count his money
   - Ⓑ eat lunch
   - Ⓒ buy a Fearless Flyer skateboard

3. What is Evan upset about?
   - Ⓐ He wants a job delivering newspapers.
   - Ⓑ He wants his own room.
   - ● He does all the chores by himself.

4. At the end of the play, Evan's parents say they will _____.
   - Ⓐ give Evan his own room
   - ● make some changes
   - Ⓒ hire a baby sitter

28   Stuck in the Middle   Leveled Readers' Theater • EMC 3483 • © Evan-Moor Corp.

Page 29

Vocabulary Activity

Name _____

I Know the Words

Fill in the circle next to the correct answer.

1. The word **deliver** can mean _____
   - Ⓐ to see   ● to bring   Ⓒ to write

2. A **hardworking** person _____
   - Ⓐ hardly works   Ⓑ works a little   ● works a lot

3. A **neighborhood** is a place with _____
   - Ⓐ one house   ● many houses   Ⓒ no houses

4. A **downtown** area usually has _____
   - Ⓐ many houses   Ⓑ a forest   ● stores and offices

5. If you are doing **chores**, you are _____.
   - Ⓐ watching TV   ● doing small jobs   Ⓒ talking on the phone

6. If you take something to the **curb**, you take it to the _____
   - Ⓐ dentist   Ⓑ backyard   ● edge of the sidewalk

© Evan-Moor Corp. • EMC 3483 • Leveled Readers' Theater   Stuck in the Middle   29

Page 30

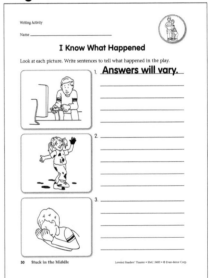

Writing Activity

Name _____

I Know What Happened

Look at each picture. Write sentences to tell what happened in the play.

1. **Answers will vary.**

2. _____

3. _____

30   Stuck in the Middle   Leveled Readers' Theater • EMC 3483 • © Evan-Moor Corp.

Page 42

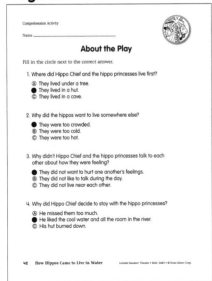

Comprehension Activity

Name _____

About the Play

Fill in the circle next to the correct answer.

1. Where did Hippo Chief and the hippo princesses live first?
   - Ⓐ They lived under a tree.
   - ● They lived in a hut.
   - Ⓒ They lived in a cave.

2. Why did the hippos want to live somewhere else?
   - ● They were too crowded.
   - Ⓑ They were too cold.
   - Ⓒ They were too hot.

3. Why didn't Hippo Chief and the hippo princesses talk to each other about how they were feeling?
   - ● They did not want to hurt one another's feelings.
   - Ⓑ They did not like to talk during the day.
   - Ⓒ They did not live near each other.

4. Why did Hippo Chief decide to stay with the hippo princesses?
   - Ⓐ He missed them too much.
   - ● He liked the cool water and all the room in the river.
   - Ⓒ His hut burned down.

42   How Hippos Came to Live in Water   Leveled Readers' Theater • EMC 3483 • © Evan-Moor Corp.

Page 43

Vocabulary Activity

Name _____

I Know the Words

Fill in the circle next to the correct answer.

1. To **overhear** something means to _____
   - Ⓐ see it   Ⓑ know it   ● hear it

2. To **search** for something means to _____
   - Ⓐ ask for it   ● look for it   Ⓒ reach for it

3. If something is **mighty**, it is _____
   - ● powerful   Ⓑ weak   Ⓒ tiny

4. If something is **tugging**, it is _____
   - Ⓐ talking   ● pulling   Ⓒ yelling

5. When you **squeeze** something, you _____
   - Ⓐ hold it gently   Ⓑ step on it   ● press it firmly

6. To be a **chief** means to be _____
   - Ⓐ a student   ● a leader   Ⓒ an animal

© Evan-Moor Corp. • EMC 3483 • Leveled Readers' Theater   How Hippos Came to Live in Water   43

Page 44

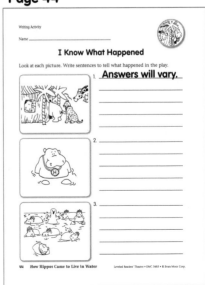

Writing Activity

Name _____

I Know What Happened

Look at each picture. Write sentences to tell what happened in the play.

1. **Answers will vary.**

2. _____

3. _____

44   How Hippos Came to Live in Water   Leveled Readers' Theater • EMC 3483 • © Evan-Moor Corp.

Page 56

Comprehension Activity

Name _____

About the Play

Fill in the circle next to the correct answer.

1. What is the main problem in the play?
   - Ⓐ The king is always having fun.
   - Ⓑ The fiddlers will not play music.
   - ● The king never laughs or smiles.

2. The queen took the king to visit _____.
   - Ⓐ the fiddlers
   - ● the jester
   - Ⓒ the doctor

3. Who did the jester call for help?
   - ● the fools
   - Ⓑ the queen
   - Ⓒ the fiddlers

4. What finally made the king laugh and smile?
   - Ⓐ the jester's jokes
   - ● the thought of the fools taking care of the kingdom
   - Ⓒ the thought of the queen taking care of the kingdom

56 Young King Cole

Leveled Readers' Theater • EMC 3483 • © Evan-Moor Corp.

Page 57

Vocabulary Activity

Name _____

I Know the Words

Fill in the circle next to the correct answer.

1. If you **howled** with laughter, you laughed _____.
   - ● very loudly
   - Ⓑ quietly
   - Ⓒ through your nose

2. The word **instead** means _____.
   - Ⓐ wrong
   - Ⓑ the same
   - ● in place of

3. You **laugh** when you think something is _____.
   - Ⓐ sad
   - ● funny
   - Ⓒ scary

4. You **swallow** after you _____.
   - ● chew
   - Ⓑ bake
   - Ⓒ cut

5. You **yawn** when you are _____.
   - Ⓐ happy
   - ● tired
   - Ⓒ sad

6. You eat **breakfast** in the _____.
   - Ⓐ evening
   - Ⓑ afternoon
   - ● morning

© Evan-Moor Corp. • EMC 3483 • Leveled Readers' Theater

Young King Cole 57

Page 58

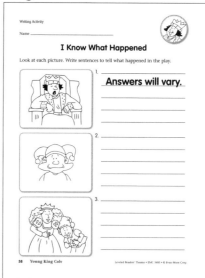

Writing Activity

Name _____

I Know What Happened

Look at each picture. Write sentences to tell what happened in the play.

1. **Answers will vary.**

2. _____

3. _____

58 Young King Cole

Leveled Readers' Theater • EMC 3483 • © Evan-Moor Corp.

Page 70

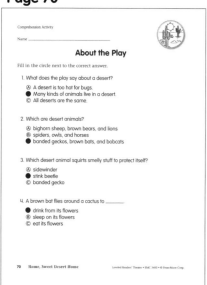

Comprehension Activity

Name _____

About the Play

Fill in the circle next to the correct answer.

1. What does the play say about a desert?
   - Ⓐ A desert is too hot for bugs.
   - ● Many kinds of animals live in a desert.
   - Ⓒ All deserts are the same.

2. Which are desert animals?
   - Ⓐ bighorn sheep, brown bears, and lions
   - Ⓑ spiders, owls, and horses
   - ● banded geckos, brown bats, and bobcats

3. Which desert animal squirts smelly stuff to protect itself?
   - Ⓐ sidewinder
   - ● stink beetle
   - Ⓒ banded gecko

4. A brown bat flies around a cactus to _____.
   - ● drink from its flowers
   - Ⓑ sleep on its flowers
   - Ⓒ eat its flowers

70 Home, Sweet Desert Home

Leveled Readers' Theater • EMC 3483 • © Evan-Moor Corp.

Page 71

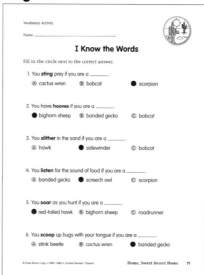

Vocabulary Activity

Name _____

I Know the Words

Fill in the circle next to the correct answer.

1. You **sting** prey if you are a _____.
   - Ⓐ cactus wren
   - Ⓑ bobcat
   - ● scorpion

2. You have **hooves** if you are a _____.
   - ● bighorn sheep
   - Ⓑ banded gecko
   - Ⓒ bobcat

3. You **slither** in the sand if you are a _____.
   - Ⓐ hawk
   - ● sidewinder
   - Ⓒ bobcat

4. You **listen** for the sound of food if you are a _____.
   - Ⓐ banded gecko
   - ● screech owl
   - Ⓒ scorpion

5. You **soar** as you hunt if you are a _____.
   - ● red-tailed hawk
   - Ⓑ bighorn sheep
   - Ⓒ roadrunner

6. You **scoop** up bugs with your tongue if you are a _____.
   - Ⓐ stink beetle
   - Ⓑ cactus wren
   - ● banded gecko

© Evan-Moor Corp. • EMC 3483 • Leveled Readers' Theater

Home, Sweet Desert Home 71

Page 72

Comprehension Activity

Name _____

I Know What Happened

Draw one desert animal in each box. Write about each animal on the lines.

1. **Answers will vary.**

2. _____

3. _____

72 Home, Sweet Desert Home

Leveled Readers' Theater • EMC 3483 • © Evan-Moor Corp.

Page 84

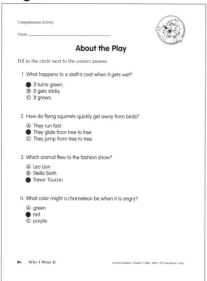

Comprehension Activity

Name _____

About the Play

Fill in the circle next to the correct answer.

1. What happens to a sloth's coat when it gets wet?
   - ● It turns green.
   - Ⓑ It gets sticky.
   - Ⓒ It grows.

2. How do flying squirrels quickly get away from birds?
   - Ⓐ They run fast.
   - ● They glide from tree to tree.
   - Ⓒ They jump from tree to tree.

3. Which animal flew to the fashion show?
   - Ⓐ Leo Lion
   - Ⓑ Stella Sloth
   - ● Trevor Toucan

4. What color might a chameleon be when it is angry?
   - Ⓐ green
   - ● red
   - Ⓒ purple

84 Why I Wear It

Leveled Readers' Theater • EMC 3483 • © Evan-Moor Corp.

Page 85

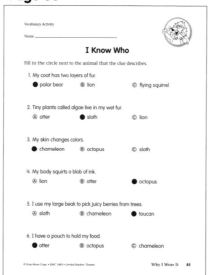

Vocabulary Activity

Name _____

I Know Who

Fill in the circle next to the animal that the clue describes.

1. My coat has two layers of fur.
   - ● polar bear
   - Ⓑ lion
   - Ⓒ flying squirrel

2. Tiny plants called algae live in my wet fur.
   - Ⓐ otter
   - ● sloth
   - Ⓒ lion

3. My skin changes colors.
   - ● chameleon
   - Ⓑ octopus
   - Ⓒ sloth

4. My body squirts a blob of ink.
   - Ⓐ lion
   - Ⓑ otter
   - ● octopus

5. I use my large beak to pick juicy berries from trees.
   - Ⓐ sloth
   - Ⓑ chameleon
   - ● toucan

6. I have a pouch to hold my food.
   - ● otter
   - Ⓑ octopus
   - Ⓒ chameleon

© Evan-Moor Corp. • EMC 3483 • Leveled Readers' Theater

Why I Wear It 85

Page 86

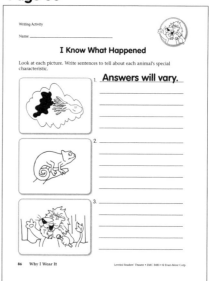

Writing Activity

Name _____

I Know What Happened

Look at each picture. Write sentences to tell about each animal's special characteristic.

1. **Answers will vary.**

2. _____

3. _____

86 Why I Wear It

Leveled Readers' Theater • EMC 3483 • © Evan-Moor Corp.

Page 96

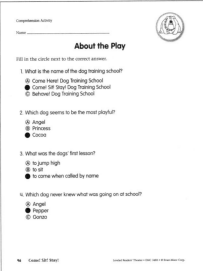

Comprehension Activity

Name _____

About the Play

Fill in the circle next to the correct answer.

1. What is the name of the dog training school?
   - Ⓐ Come Here! Dog Training School
   - ● Come! Sit! Stay! Dog Training School
   - Ⓒ Behave! Dog Training School

2. Which dog seems to be the most playful?
   - Ⓐ Angel
   - Ⓑ Princess
   - ● Cocoa

3. What was the dogs' first lesson?
   - Ⓐ to jump high
   - Ⓑ to sit
   - ● to come when called by name

4. Which dog never knew what was going on at school?
   - Ⓐ Angel
   - ● Pepper
   - Ⓒ Gonzo

96   Come! Sit! Stay!   Leveled Readers' Theater • EMC 3483 • © Evan-Moor Corp.

Page 97

Vocabulary Activity

Name _____

I Know the Words

Fill in the circle next to the correct answer.

1. If something is **pleasant**, it is _____.
   - Ⓐ mean
   - Ⓑ sad
   - ● nice

2. If something is **elegant**, it is _____.
   - ● fancy
   - Ⓑ dull
   - Ⓒ wet

3. If dogs are **trampling** flowers, they are _____.
   - Ⓐ smelling them
   - ● walking on them
   - Ⓒ looking at them

4. If dogs are making a **ruckus**, they are _____.
   - Ⓐ behaving
   - ● making noise
   - Ⓒ sleeping

5. The word **nuttin'** is slang for the word _____.
   - Ⓐ nuts
   - Ⓑ nobody
   - ● nothing

6. The word **whadd'ya** is slang for the words _____.
   - ● what do you
   - Ⓑ who are you
   - Ⓒ when did you

© Evan-Moor Corp. • EMC 3483 • Leveled Readers' Theater   Come! Sit! Stay!   97

Page 98

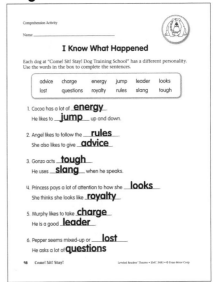

Comprehension Activity

Name _____

I Know What Happened

Each dog at "Come! Sit! Stay! Dog Training School" has a different personality. Use the words in the box to complete the sentences.

| advice | charge | energy | jump | leader | looks |
| lost | questions | royalty | rules | slang | tough |

1. Cocoa has a lot of **energy**
   He likes to **jump** up and down.

2. Angel likes to follow the **rules**
   She also likes to give **advice**

3. Gonzo acts **tough**
   He uses **slang** when he speaks.

4. Princess pays a lot of attention to how she **looks**
   She thinks she looks like **royalty**

5. Murphy likes to take **charge**
   He is a good **leader**

6. Pepper seems mixed-up or **lost**
   He asks a lot of **questions**

98   Come! Sit! Stay!   Leveled Readers' Theater • EMC 3483 • © Evan-Moor Corp.

Page 110

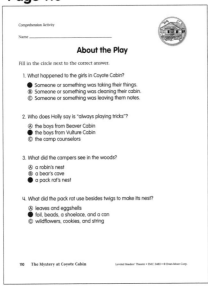

Comprehension Activity

Name _____

About the Play

Fill in the circle next to the correct answer.

1. What happened to the girls in Coyote Cabin?
   - ● Someone or something was taking their things.
   - Ⓑ Someone or something was cleaning their cabin.
   - Ⓒ Someone or something was leaving them notes.

2. Who does Holly say is "always playing tricks"?
   - Ⓐ the boys from Beaver Cabin
   - ● the boys from Vulture Cabin
   - Ⓒ the camp counselors

3. What did the campers see in the woods?
   - Ⓐ a robin's nest
   - Ⓑ a bear's cave
   - ● a pack rat's nest

4. What did the pack rat use besides twigs to make its nest?
   - Ⓐ leaves and eggshells
   - ● foil, beads, a shoelace, and a can
   - Ⓒ wildflowers, cookies, and string

110   The Mystery at Coyote Cabin   Leveled Readers' Theater • EMC 3483 • © Evan-Moor Corp.

Page 111

Vocabulary Activity

Name _____

I Know the Words

Fill in the circle next to the correct answer.

1. If something **occurred**, it _____.
   - ● happened
   - Ⓑ did not happen
   - Ⓒ might happen

2. If something is a **mystery**, it is _____.
   - Ⓐ new
   - ● unexplained
   - Ⓒ known

3. If you are **roasting** something, you are _____.
   - ● cooking it
   - Ⓑ making it
   - Ⓒ throwing it

4. If something is **pitch-dark**, it is _____.
   - Ⓐ not dark
   - ● very dark
   - Ⓒ very light

5. When you **donate** something, you _____.
   - Ⓐ buy it
   - Ⓑ sell it
   - ● give it away

6. What does it mean to **accidentally** do something?
   - Ⓐ do it at night
   - ● do it by mistake
   - Ⓒ do it on purpose

© Evan-Moor Corp. • EMC 3483 • Leveled Readers' Theater   The Mystery at Coyote Cabin   111

Page 112

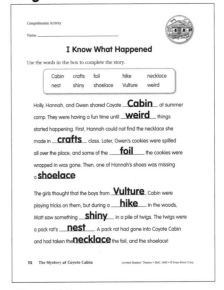

Comprehension Activity

Name _____

I Know What Happened

Use the words in the box to complete the story.

| Cabin | crafts | foil | hike | necklace |
| nest | shiny | shoelace | Vulture | weird |

Holly, Hannah, and Gwen shared Coyote **Cabin** at summer camp. They were having a fun time until **weird** things started happening. First, Hannah could not find the necklace she made in **crafts** class. Later, Gwen's cookies were spilled all over the place, and some of the **foil** the cookies were wrapped in was gone. Then, one of Hannah's shoes was missing a **shoelace**

The girls thought that the boys from **Vulture** Cabin were playing tricks on them, but during a **hike** in the woods, Matt saw something **shiny** in a pile of twigs. The twigs were a pack rat's **nest** A pack rat had gone into Coyote Cabin and had taken the **necklace** the foil, and the shoelace!

112   The Mystery at Coyote Cabin   Leveled Readers' Theater • EMC 3483 • © Evan-Moor Corp.

Page 122

Comprehension Activity

Name _____

About the Play

Fill in the circle next to the correct answer.

1. Where is the Quangle Wangle Quee?
   - Ⓐ in a house
   - ● in the Crumpetty Tree
   - Ⓒ in an oak tree

2. Why can't anyone see the Quangle Wangle's face?
   - ● He wears a big hat.
   - Ⓑ His hair is too long.
   - Ⓒ He doesn't have a face.

3. What is the best food for the Quangle Wangle Quee?
   - Ⓐ butter and jelly
   - Ⓑ jam and eggs
   - ● jam, jelly, and bread

4. What did the animals want to build on the Quangle Wangle's hat?
   - ● their homes
   - Ⓑ a barn
   - Ⓒ tables and chairs

5. What sound did all the animals dance to?
   - Ⓐ the screeching of a Bisky Bat
   - ● the flute of the blue baboon
   - Ⓒ the chirping of Mr. and Mrs. Canary

122   Quangle Wangle Quee   Leveled Readers' Theater • EMC 3483 • © Evan-Moor Corp.

Page 123

Vocabulary Activity

Name _____

I Know the Words

Fill in the circle next to the correct answer.

1. If a place is **airy**, it has _____.
   - Ⓐ no space
   - ● a lot of space
   - Ⓒ very little space

2. The word **luminous** means _____.
   - Ⓐ noisy
   - Ⓑ small
   - ● shining

3. The phrase **on account of** means _____.
   - Ⓐ instead of
   - ● because of
   - Ⓒ besides

4. The word **creatures** is another word for _____.
   - Ⓐ hats
   - Ⓑ trees
   - ● animals

5. The word **plain** means _____.
   - ● ordinary
   - Ⓑ busy
   - Ⓒ loud

© Evan-Moor Corp. • EMC 3483 • Leveled Readers' Theater   Quangle Wangle Quee   123

Page 124

Writing Activity

Name _____

I Know What Happened

Look at each picture. Write sentences to tell what happened in the play.

1. **Answers will vary.**
_____
_____
_____

2. _____
_____
_____

3. _____
_____
_____

124   Quangle Wangle Quee   Leveled Readers' Theater • EMC 3483 • © Evan-Moor Corp.

© Evan-Moor Corp. • EMC 3483 • Leveled Readers' Theater

Page 136

Comprehension Activity

Name _____

About the Play

Fill in the circle next to the correct answer.

1. Where did Gloria learn about "going green"?
   - Ⓐ at school
   - ● at summer camp
   - Ⓒ at her friend's house

2. What did Gloria buy at the dollar store?
   - Ⓐ candy
   - Ⓑ paper bags
   - ● reusable water bottles

3. What did Gloria make for Gavin?
   - ● cookies
   - Ⓑ vegetables
   - Ⓒ corn chips

4. Why was the food Gloria cooked "eco-friendly"?
   - Ⓐ It was from her garden.
   - ● It was homemade and had no cardboard or plastic packaging.
   - Ⓒ It was green in color.

136   Going Green   Leveled Readers' Theater • EMC 3483 • © Evan-Moor Corp.

Page 137

Vocabulary Activity

Name _____

I Know the Words

Fill in the circle next to the correct answer.

1. The word **reuse** means to _____.
   - ● use again
   - Ⓑ eat quickly
   - Ⓒ not use again

2. The word **eco-friendly** means _____.
   - Ⓐ bad for Earth
   - ● good for Earth
   - Ⓒ made from earth

3. The word **definitely** means _____.
   - Ⓐ maybe
   - ● for sure
   - Ⓒ probably

4. The word **conserving** means _____.
   - Ⓐ wasting
   - Ⓑ using up
   - ● using carefully

5. The word **disgusting** means _____.
   - ● yucky
   - Ⓑ yummy
   - Ⓒ young

© Evan-Moor Corp. • EMC 3483 • Leveled Readers' Theater   Going Green   137

Page 138

Writing Activity

Name _____

I Know What Happened

Look at each picture. Write sentences to tell what happened in the play.

1. **Answers will vary.**

2. _____

3. _____

138   Going Green   Leveled Readers' Theater • EMC 3483 • © Evan-Moor Corp.

Page 152

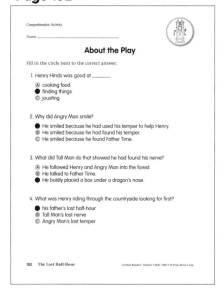

Comprehension Activity

Name _____

About the Play

Fill in the circle next to the correct answer.

1. Henry Hinds was good at _____.
   - Ⓐ cooking food
   - ● finding things
   - Ⓒ jousting

2. Why did Angry Man smile?
   - ● He smiled because he had used his temper to help Henry.
   - Ⓑ He smiled because he had found his temper.
   - Ⓒ He smiled because he found Father Time.

3. What did Tall Man do that showed he had found his nerve?
   - Ⓐ He followed Henry and Angry Man into the forest.
   - Ⓑ He talked to Father Time.
   - ● He boldly placed a box under a dragon's nose.

4. What was Henry riding through the countryside looking for first?
   - ● his father's lost half-hour
   - Ⓑ Tall Man's lost nerve
   - Ⓒ Angry Man's lost temper

152   The Lost Half-Hour   Leveled Readers' Theater • EMC 3483 • © Evan-Moor Corp.

Page 153

Vocabulary Activity

Name _____

I Know the Words

Fill in the circle next to the correct answer.

1. To have **nerve** means to have _____.
   - Ⓐ fear
   - ● courage
   - Ⓒ a metal suit

2. To **quiver** means to _____.
   - Ⓐ jump
   - Ⓑ sleep
   - ● shake

3. To **drift** means to _____.
   - Ⓐ sit still
   - Ⓑ roll in the dirt
   - ● be carried along by air

4. To **explode** means to _____.
   - Ⓐ hide
   - ● blow up
   - Ⓒ ride a horse

5. When you lose your **temper**, you are _____.
   - Ⓐ scared
   - ● angry
   - Ⓒ happy

6. What would you see in the **countryside**?
   - ● hills and trees
   - Ⓑ many houses
   - Ⓒ tall buildings

© Evan-Moor Corp. • EMC 3483 • Leveled Readers' Theater   The Lost Half-Hour   153

Page 154

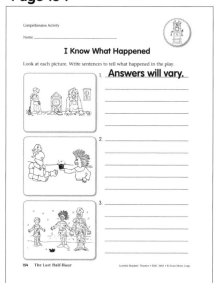

Comprehension Activity

Name _____

I Know What Happened

Look at each picture. Write sentences to tell what happened in the play.

1. **Answers will vary.**

2. _____

3. _____

154   The Lost Half-Hour   Leveled Readers' Theater • EMC 3483 • © Evan-Moor Corp.

Read and Understand

The perfect comprehensive resource to supplement your core reading program! Motivating reading selections accompanied by comprehension and vocabulary activities make *Read and Understand* a must-have resource for providing students with extra reading practice and test prep. 144 pages. **Correlated to state standards.**

Each Read and Understand *title includes:*

- *19 to 23 reproducible stories or poems*
- *multiple activity pages to practice comprehension, vocabulary, and other vital language arts skills*
- *engaging illustrations that support the text*

Story pages

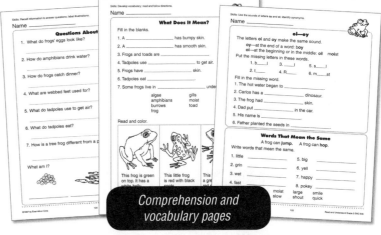

Comprehension and vocabulary pages

Read and Understand
Stories and Activities

Grade K	EMC 637-PRO
Grade 1	EMC 638-PRO
Grade 2	EMC 639-PRO
Grade 3	EMC 640-PRO

Fiction
Grades 4–6+	EMC 748-PRO

Nonfiction
Grades 4–6+	EMC 749-PRO

More Read and Understand
Stories and Activities

Grade 1	EMC 745-PRO
Grade 2	EMC 746-PRO
Grade 3	EMC 747-PRO

Read and Understand
Poetry

Grades 2–3	EMC 3323-PRO
Grades 3–4	EMC 3324-PRO
Grades 4–5	EMC 3325-PRO
Grades 5–6+	EMC 3326-PRO

Read and Understand
Literature Genres

Fairy Tales & Folktales
Grades 1–2	EMC 756-PRO

Folktales & Fables
Grades 2–3	EMC 757-PRO

Tall Tales
Grades 3–4	EMC 758-PRO

Myths & Legends
Grades 4–6+	EMC 759-PRO

Read and Understand
Science

Grades 1–2	EMC 3302-PRO
Grades 2–3	EMC 3303-PRO
Grades 3–4	EMC 3304-PRO
Grades 4–6+	EMC 3305-PRO

Preview at
www.evan-moor.com

Language Fundamentals

Your comprehensive resource for reproducible grade-level grammar, mechanics, and usage practice.

Target the specific language skills your students need to practice most with over 160 student activity pages, scaffolded to accommodate students' various skill levels. Review pages in test format are perfect for test prep, while sentence- and paragraph-editing exercises provide students with a real-world application of skills. 240 reproducible pages. ***Correlated to state standards.***

Grade 1	EMC 2751-PRO
Grade 2	EMC 2752-PRO
Grade 3	EMC 2753-PRO
Grade 4	EMC 2754-PRO
Grade 5	EMC 2755-PRO
Grade 6+	EMC 2756-PRO

Covers the same skills as *Daily Language Review!*

Literature Pockets

Add hands-on, active learning experiences to your literature studies using award-winning reading, writing, and art projects! The easy-to-make "pockets" in each *Literature Pockets* book are perfect for creating a comprehensive portfolio of student work. Each pocket lesson focuses on a literature genre or genre-specific story. It's the perfect way to extend your literature studies! 96 reproducible pages. ***Correlated to state standards.***

Provide students with engaging, hands-on literature practice using...

- *motivating 3D art projects*
- *easy-to-follow teacher directions*
- *illustrated covers and labels for each pocket*
- *interesting and helpful background information*

Folktales & Fairy Tales
Grades K–1   EMC 2730-PRO

Nursery Rhymes*
Grades K–1   EMC 2700-PRO

Caldecott Winners*
Grades 1–3   EMC 2701-PRO

Folktales & Fairy Tales
Grades 2–3   EMC 2731-PRO

Aesop's Fables
Grades 2–3   EMC 2733-PRO

Caldecott Winners*
Grades 4–6+   EMC 2702-PRO

Fiction*
Grades 4–6+   EMC 2703-PRO

Greek & Roman Myths
Grades 4–6+   EMC 2734-PRO

Nonfiction*
Grades 4–6+   EMC 2704-PRO

Tall Tales
Grades 4–6+   EMC 2732-PRO

** *Learning*® Magazine Teachers' Choice Award*